Slashing Your Taxes:

83 Tax Saving Tips Which Can Save You Thousands of Dollars

Danny Fink, CPA

DANNY FINK

Slashing Your Taxes:

83 Tax Saving Tips Which Can Save You Thousands of Dollars

Danny Fink, CPA

www.premiertaxresolution.com
info@premiertaxresolution.com
(888)505-6592

Business & Money > Taxation > Small Business
Professional & Technical > Law > Practical Guide

Copyright © 2014 Danny Fink

All rights reserved.

ISBN: 10:1502886529
ISBN-13:978-1502886521

DEDICATION

Dedicated to my boys, Alex and Ben. You are the best.

IMPORTANT NOTICE

While every effort has been taken to ensure that the information contained herein is accurate as of the time of publication, tax laws and regulations are constantly changing.

This book is designed to provide accurate and authoritative information in regards to the subject matter covered, but it is sold with the understanding that the publisher is not engaged in legal services, and no information contained herein should be construed as legal advice.

If legal or other assistance is required, the services of a competent professional person should be sought. The publisher does not guarantee or warrant that readers who use the information provided in this publication will achieve results similar to those discussed.

NOTICE: To ensure compliance with requirements imposed by the IRS, we inform you that any US federal tax advice contained in this book is not intended or written to be used, and cannot be used, for the purposes of (i) avoiding penalties under the Internal Revenue Code, or (ii) promoting marketing or recommending to another party any tax related matter addressed herein.

CONTENTS

1. Standard Deduction — 5
2. Itemized Deductions — 8
3. Earned Income Tax Credit — 10
4. The American Opportunity Tax Credit — 13
5. Lifetime Learning Credit — 18
6. Student Loan Interest Deduction — 20
7. Tuition and Fees Deduction — 22
8. Work Related Education — 24
9. Child-Care Credit — 26
10. Child-Care Credit for Part-Time Workers — 29
11. Child-Care Credit for Students — 31
12. Child-Care Credit for Camps — 32
13. Child and Dependent Care Credit — 33
14. Child Tax Credit — 34
15. Excess Social Security and RRTA Tax Withheld — 35
16. Retirement Savings Contributions Credit — 37
17. Tax Deduction for Traditional IRA Contribution — 39
18. Contribute to an IRA Even if Covered by another Retirement Plan — 41
19. Home Mortgage Interest – Not Just First Mortgage — 43

20. Home Mortgage Interest – To Finance Car Purchase ... 44

21. Home Mortgage Interest – Pay off Credit Card Debt ... 46

22. Home Mortgage Interest – Not Just For Houses ... 47

23. Medical and Dental Expenses ... 48

24. Medical and Dental Expenses – Transportation/Travel ... 50

25. Medical and Dental Expenses – Weight Loss ... 52

26. Medical and Dental Expenses – Medical Insurance Premiums ... 53

27. Medical and Dental Expenses – Long Term care Insurance ... 54

28. Medical and Dental Expenses – Capital Expenditures ... 55

29. Health Insurance Premium Tax Credits ... 57

30. State and Local Income Taxes ... 58

31. State and Local Sales Taxes ... 60

32. Real Estate Taxes ... 62

33. Personal Property Taxes ... 63

34. Pet Expenses ... 64

35. Moving Expenses ... 65

36. Charitable Contributions ... 67

37. Large Contributions ... 68

38. Cash or Check Contributions ... 69

39. Non-Cash or Check Contributions	70
40. Contributions When You Received Benefits	71
41. Volunteer Mileage	73
42. Volunteer Uniform Costs	74
43. Miscellaneous Deductions	75
44. Tax Preparation Fees	77
45. Unreimbursed Employee Expenses - General	78
46. Business Liability Insurance	80
47. Depreciation on Computers	81
48. Professional Dues	82
49. Educator Expenses	83
50. Job Search Expenses	85
51. Legal Fees	87
52. Licenses and Regulatory Fees	88
53. Occupational Taxes	89
54. Research Expenses of a College Professor	90
55. Tools Used in Your Work	91
56. Travel	92
57. Local Transportation Expenses	93
58. Travel from Your Home Office	94
59. Meals and Entertainment	95
60. Gift Expenses	96

61. Home-Office Deduction – If you are an Employee	97
62. Local Lodging	98
63. Union Dues	99
64. Work Clothes and Uniforms	100
65. Protective Clothing	101
66. Gambling Losses	102
67. Selected Business Deductions	103
68. Business Expenses vs. Personal Expenses	107
69. Passive Losses	108
70. Capital Expenses	110
71. Business Expenses That Are Deductible	111
72. Advertising	114
73. Office Expense	115
74. Supplies	116
75. Taxes and licenses	117
76. Self-Employed Health Insurance Deduction	118
77. Home-Office Deduction if Self Employed	120
78. Car and Truck Expenses – Self Employed	140
79. Parking fees and tolls	146
80. Travel, Meals, and Entertainment	147
81. Meals	149

82. Trip Primarily for Personal Reasons — 152
83. Entertainment — 153
84. Conclusion — 155

DANNY FINK

INTRODUCTION

First I want to thank you for purchasing my book, "Slashing Your Taxes: 83 Tax Saving Tips Which Can Save You Thousands of Dollars". The purpose of this book is to help you legally minimize the amount of taxes you pay. The US Tax Code is thousands of pages long and very complex. Not even the most knowledgeable tax expert knows everything. Obviously, I'm not going to be able to cover every tax topic. What I want to try to do is provide you with a resource that gives you information on the topics most likely to save you money on your taxes.

I also want to point out that I am not suggesting in any that you inflate the amount of your deductions or claim deductions or credits that you don't qualify for. However, I do want you to have the knowledge to take full advantage of the deductions and credits that you legitimately qualify for.

I'm not going to simply list the various credits and deductions available. I want to provide you with some of the types of expenses that can be included under the various deduction or credit categories. I'll also provide numerous examples to show you how the deduction or credit can impact the amount of tax you pay. Also, for selected topics I'll provide statistical information from the IRS about the deduction or credit, including how many people claimed the deduction or credit, and what the average deduction or credit amount was.

I'll also try to group similar types of deductions or credits together. For example I'll discuss all of the various education related credits and deductions one after the other. This should help you if you are trying to research a specific topic.

For the most part I'm going to talk about tax credits before covering tax deductions, just because tax credits are more valuable than tax deductions. With tax credits, for each dollar of credit, you save a dollar in taxes. With a tax deduction, each dollar of deduction is multiplied by your tax rate to get your tax savings. If you are in the 25% tax bracket, each dollar in deductions is worth 25 cents in tax savings, if you are in the 15% tax bracket each dollar in deductions would save you 15 cents.

I want to put the most valuable tips early in the book so that you are more likely to see them in case you don't read the entire book.

I want to provide you with some statistics from the IRS Statistics of Income Bulletin. You may be wondering what the most common deduction or tax credit is, or maybe you are curious about which deduction or credit provides the largest benefit on average to those taxpayers who claim it.

This information won't necessarily help you to reduce your taxes, but I thought you may find it interesting. I also want to use it to demonstrate how the most common deduction may not be the most valuable deduction or credit, depending on your particular circumstances.

The single most common tax deduction is the Standard deduction, 66.4 percent of all tax returns filed in 2011 used the Standard deduction, with an additional nine percent claiming the standard deduction then adding in additional deductions in the margin of their return. The IRS considers those with additions to the standard deduction to be itemized returns. Some simple math tells us that any single itemized deduction can be claimed by no more than 33.6 percent of taxpayers since 66.4 percent used the Standard deduction. Most of the itemized deductions will be claimed by far fewer than 33 percent of taxpayers since not everyone claims every itemized deduction.

The most common itemized deduction was the deduction for real estate taxes paid, with 27.6 of all taxpayers claiming the deduction, this is 81.6 percent of all itemized returns.

The second most common itemized deduction was the home mortgage interest deduction, with 24.4 percent of all returns claiming the deduction, or 72.6 percent of all itemized returns.

Next on the list is the deduction for charitable contributions. Of all returns filed, 23.7 percent claimed this deduction, or 70 percent of itemized returns.

Now let's look at which deductions are the most valuable on average for those taxpayers who claimed the deduction.

Number one this list, is the deduction for gambling losses, while less than one percent of all returns claimed this deduction, the average deduction amount for those who claimed it was over $19,500.

The second most valuable itemized deduction was the home mortgage interest deduction, with an average deduction amount of just over $10,000.

Next was the medical and dental expense deduction, coming in with an average deduction of over $8,100 even after meeting the 7.5

percent of AGI threshold.

Now let's take a look at the top tax credits.

The most popular tax credit was the Earned Income Credit, with 19.3 percent of all returns claiming this credit.

The second most popular tax credit was the Child Tax Credit, with 15.8 percent claiming the credit.

As for the most valuable tax credit, the Earned Income Credit and the Child Tax Credit again finished first and second, with average credit amounts of $2,254 and $1,215 respectively.

With all of that being said let's get started.

1. STANDARD DEDUCTION

Most people who file a tax return must decide whether to take the standard deduction or to itemize their deductions on Schedule A. Of course you want to get the largest deduction available to you, so unless you know for sure that the standard deduction is going to be larger than if you itemize, I suggest preparing Schedule A, then comparing your itemized deduction amount to the standard deduction amount. Obviously, you then choose the method that gives you the largest deduction.

According to the IRS Statistics of Income Bulletin for 2011, which is the most recent data available at the time of writing, just over 145 million individual tax returns were filed in the United States, of those, two-thirds or about 96.5 million taxpayers choose to claim the standard deduction. An additional nine percent, or 13.2 million taxpayers, choose the standard deduction, and then wrote in an additional amount in the margin of their tax return. This accounts for 75 percent of all individual tax returns filed for the year.

The standard deduction is adjusted each year to account for inflation and also varies depending on your filing status. Your standard deduction consists of the basic standard deduction and any additional standard deduction for being age 65 and over and for blindness. For 2014 the standard deduction is $6,200 for single taxpayers and married taxpayers filing separately. While the standard deduction is $12,400 for married couples filing jointly, and $9,100 for heads of household.

As I mentioned earlier, the standard deduction is increased for taxpayers over 65 years of age, or who are blind. For example, the standard deduction for a 65 year old taxpayer is $7,700, and $9,200 for those who are 65 or over and blind. I'm not going to list all the different standard deductions for all of the various possibilities here. I just wanted to make you aware that the standard deduction is increased for these taxpayers.

If you or your spouse can be claimed as a dependent on another person's tax return, your standard deduction is generally limited to the greater of $1,000 or your earned income for the year, plus $350. But it can't be more than the regular standard deduction amount of $6,200.

It should be noted that not everyone is eligible for the standard deduction and must therefore itemize their deductions. One such case is, if you are married and file separately and your spouse itemizes deductions on their return, then you must also itemize deductions on your return. If you think about it, this makes sense. Let me give an example, let's say a couple has $15,000 in itemized deductions. If they file married filing jointly, the $15,000 is the total amount of deductions they could claim. But, if they were allowed to have one spouse itemize while the other took the standard deduction, one spouse could take the $15,000 in itemized deductions, while the other took their $6,200 standard deduction giving them an additional $6,200 in deductions compared to if they had filed jointly.

Two other situations where the standard deduction is not allowed is if you are filing a tax return for a short tax year because of a change in your annual accounting period, or if you are a nonresident or dual-status alien during the year.

If you don't itemize you deductions and later realize that you should have or conversely, if you itemize and later discover that you should have taken the standard deduction, you can file an amended return to make the change. This is done by filing Form 1040X.

2. ITEMIZED DEDUCTIONS

We have looked briefly at the standard deduction, later we will look at some of the deductions that are used to compute your total itemized deductions. As I mentioned in the previous section, 66 percent of taxpayers choose the standard deduction, leaving 34 percent who itemize. For those who choose to itemize, their total deductions averaged $25,980 in 2011 according to IRS data. This is much higher than the standard deduction, which is logical, as only those who had itemized deductions totaling more than the standard deduction would choose to itemize.

I do want to point out that there is a limitation for itemized deductions for higher income taxpayers. For 2014 the threshold amounts are: $305,050 for married filing jointly and qualifying widow(er); $152,525 if married filing separately; $279,650 for head of household; and $254,200 if single.

Once a taxpayer's adjusted gross income exceeds the threshold amount for their filing status, the total amount of itemized deductions is reduced by a certain amount. The reduction amount is the smaller of the following two amounts:

- 3% of the amount that the adjusted gross income exceeds the threshold; or

- 80% of itemized deductions except for medical expenses, investment interest, casualty and theft losses and gambling losses.

The overall limitation on itemized deductions is applied after the limit on charitable gifts and after the 2% of adjusted gross income limit on miscellaneous deduction.

While this limitation will not affect the vast majority of taxpayers it can have a significant impact for high income taxpayers. Let me give an example. Assuming a married couple has an adjusted gross income of $505,050 and the total of their state and real property taxes, mortgage interest, and charitable contributions paid in 2014 was $65,000. Since their adjusted gross income is $200,000 over the $305,050 limit for purposes of the itemized deduction phase out, this amount is then multiplied by 3 percent, resulting a reduction amount of $6,000. Their itemized deductions that are allowed to be claimed on line 40 of their Form 1040 are reduced from $65,000 to $59,000. If they are in the 35 percent tax bracket, the loss of $6,000 from their itemized deductions would result in additional tax of about $2,100.

3. EARNED INCOME TAX CREDIT

The Earned Income Tax Credit is one of the largest tax credits taxpayers can get. It is essentially for taxpayers not earning a lot of money. The reason the Earned Income Tax Credit was established was to offset the burden of Social Security taxes and to provide an incentive to work. To qualify for the Earned Income Tax Credit (EITC) you have to be between the ages of 25 and 65 and can't be claimed as a dependent on another person's return. In addition, if you are married you have to file jointly, to claim the EITC, you can't file married-filing separately.

I want to point out a common misconception about the EITC, many people think that self-employed taxpayers don't qualify for this credit. When in fact they do qualify for the credit.

On the other hand some people claim the credit when they are not eligible because they don't understand that if you have too much investment income, you don't qualify for the EITC even if your total income falls within the guidelines.

Let me give you the maximum income levels as well as the maximum credit amounts for 2014.

Earned Income and adjusted gross income (AGI) must each be

less than:

- $46,997 for single taxpayers, $52,427 for married filing jointly, with three or more qualifying children
- $43,756 for single taxpayers, $49,186 for married filing jointly, with two qualifying children
- $38,511 for single taxpayers, $43,941 for married filing jointly, with one qualifying child
- $14,590 for single taxpayers, $20,020 for married filing jointly, with no qualifying children

Tax Year 2014 maximum credit:

- $6,143 with three or more qualifying children
- $5,460 with two qualifying children
- $3,305 with one qualifying child
- $496 with no qualifying children

No matter what your total income is, your investment income has to be less than $3,350 or less for the year to qualify for the EITC.

For 2011, almost 28 million taxpayers claimed the EITC, which is about 19 percent of all returns filed. On average, each taxpayer who claimed the EIC received a credit of over $2,200.

As you can see, the credit amounts for the EITC are substantial. When you take into account that tax credits are much more valuable than tax deductions you can understand why the tax credit is a major source of tax fraud.

First let me briefly explain why a tax credit is more valuable than a tax deduction. If you have a $1,000 tax deduction and are in the 25% tax bracket, you would save $250 in taxes. However, a $1,000 tax credit actually reduces your taxes by $1,000.

I mentioned tax fraud involving the EITC a little earlier; let me explain how some taxpayers claim the EITC when they aren't eligible. Since you have to have earned income to be eligible for the credit and income from self-employment counts. People who don't have any actual earned income will claim to have fictitious small businesses. For example, they will claim to have say $20,000 in gross income from the business with $10,000 of business expenses. So they would report a net income of $10,000 from the fake "business".

You might be asking why someone would claim to have more income than they actually have. Remember, with your standard deduction and exemptions you can have a substantial amount of income before any tax is owed. So they would owe no tax on the bogus reported income, then since the Earned Income Tax Credit is refundable, they would get a big fat tax refund even if they didn't pay any tax that year.

The IRS says that between 23 and 28% of all EITC have errors, some of these may simply be honest errors, but a large amount is due to fraud. The estimated fraudulent payout in tax refunds is $13 - $16 Billion per year.

Since tax credits are so much more valuable than tax deductions, I'm going to discuss another tax credit next.

4. THE AMERICAN OPPORTUNITY TAX CREDIT

The American Opportunity Tax Credit (AOTC) used to be called the Hope Credit. The AOTC is to help taxpayers who are working toward a college degree. The AOTC covers the first four years of post-secondary education. So if you have spent four years in college completing your undergraduate degree and are now working on your Master's degree, you wouldn't be eligible for this credit.

In 2011, 12.8 million taxpayers, almost nine percent of all tax returns, claimed the AOTC according to the IRS. These taxpayers received an average of $900 in tax credit.

Depending on your income (the credit drops as income increases), you can receive up to $2,500 of the cost of qualified tuition and other course materials you paid during the taxable year. The American Opportunity credit equals 100% of the first $2,000 of a student's qualified education expenses plus 25% of the next $2,000.

The student has to be enrolled at least half-time for at least one academic period. A big advantage of this credit is that it is available on a per-student basis. That means if you have three kids in college, you can claim up to $7,500 in credits. This would be a huge tax savings.

The American Opportunity credit is phased out if your modified adjusted income (MAGI) exceeds certain levels. For single taxpayers the phase-out range is from $80,000 to $90,000. This means if your MAGI is less than $80,000 if single, you would qualify for the full credit, and if your MAGI is above $90,000 you wouldn't qualify at all. For married filing jointly, the phase-out range is $160,000 to $180,000. These income limits are higher than for the other education credit, the Lifetime Learning Credit, which we will cover later.

It is important to note that if you file married filing separately, you are not eligible for this credit regardless of your income level. So keep that in mind when determining what filing status to use if you are otherwise qualified for the credit and have educational expenses that qualify. Missing this credit simply due to choosing the wrong filing status could be very costly. As I mentioned above if you have three kids in college, the credit could be worth up to $7,500 in actual tax reduction.

Now let's take a look at what educational expenses actually qualify for the AOTC. For the American Opportunity Tax Credit, qualified expenses have been expanded to include expenditures for course materials, as well as tuition and required fees. For this purpose, the IRS has defined the term "course materials" to "include books, supplies and equipment needed for a course of study whether or not the materials are purchased from the educational institution as a condition of enrollment or attendance".

Computing the credit amount is a three-step process. The first step is adding up all of your qualified educational expenses. In step two, you have to subtract from your total qualified educational expenses any amounts you received as tax-free educational assistance during the tax year that are allocable to the particular academic period in question. Tax-free educational assistance includes:

- The tax-free part of any scholarship or fellowship;
- The tax-free part of any employer-provided educational assistance;
- Tax-free veterans' educational assistance, and
- Any other educational assistance that is excludable from gross income (tax free).

"Tax-free" assistance does **not** include a gift, bequest, devise, or inheritance. It also does not include any portion of a scholarship or fellowship that must be included in gross income.

If after making these adjustments, the amount of qualified education expenses exceeds the maximum credit of $2,500, then you can only claim the $2,500 maximum. If the amount is lower than $2,500, then you may be able to claim the whole amount, subject to the AGI phase-out of the credit.

If your AGI falls within the phase out range you need to reduce your credit amount based on where your AGI falls within the phase-out range. To do this, you subtract you AGI from the top threshold amount ($180,000 for married joint filers; $90,000 for single filers, heads of household, and qualifying widowers). Next, you divide the difference by either $20,000 for married joint filers or $10,000 for single filers, heads of household, and qualifying widowers. The resulting quotient should be multiplied by the total amount of qualified education expenses after adjustments for tax-free educational assistance. The product of that should be subtracted from the total amount of qualified education expenses, after adjustments. The result is the amount of the American Opportunity Tax Credit the taxpayer can claim.

I know that sounds complicated, and it is a little. Let me give you can example, if you are a single taxpayer with an AGI of $85,670, you would subtract that amount from the top threshold amount for single taxpayers which is $90,000. Then you would take the difference of

$4,330 and divide it by $10,000. The quotient is .433, meaning the taxpayer must reduce his American Opportunity tax credit amount by 43.3 percent. Let's assume that, the amount of your qualified education expenses, after adjustments for scholarships, was $1,600, then the total credit amount that you could claim would be $891.20 because: $1,600 − ($1,600 × .443) = **$891.20**

In addition, the credit is 40% refundable. This means that a portion of the credit will be refunded to you, even if you don't owe any tax. Like many tax topics, how this works is a little complicated. Let me give you some examples to help clarify.

Let's assume that your American Opportunity credit is $2,500. The refundable portion would be $1,000 ($2,500 x 40%). That amount would be treated the same as a payment on your tax return or as if you had the $1,000 withheld from your wages.

The remaining $1,500 ($2,500 x 60%) is a nonrefundable credit that is beneficial to you, only if you owe federal income taxes. If you don't owe any federal income tax because of deductions or other credits, the entire $1,000 refundable credit counts as a tax overpayment and would be refunded to you.

Let me give another example, if you owe $1,900 in taxes, the nonrefundable $1,500 portion of the credit is first used to reduce your tax bill to $400. Then the first $400 of the refundable credit is used to lower your tax bill to zero. Finally, the last $600 of the refundable credit is paid to you as a tax refund.

If your federal income tax owed is $4,500, the $1,500 nonrefundable portion of the credit reduces your tax to $3,000. Then the $1,000 refundable credit further reduces your tax bill to $2,000.

Whether the cost of a computer qualifies for the credit would depend on the facts. The purchase of a computer would qualify for the credit if the computer is needed as a condition of enrollment or attendance at the college. But, it wouldn't qualify if the computer was needed but not required.

I think it is important to note that the American Opportunity Tax Credit is not the only tax benefit for education. There are a couple of others. I'll mention them here and then discuss them in detail later. These are the Lifetime Learning Credit and the deduction for tuition and other college costs as part of your itemized deductions.

Since you can't claim more than one education tax benefit in the same year; you will want to calculate the effect of all three options to determine which is most beneficial in your particular situation.

5. LIFETIME LEARNING CREDIT

Like the American Opportunity Tax Credit, the Lifetime Learning Credit was also enacted to help offset the costs of post-secondary education. But there are some significant differences in the two education credits, especially in regards to who qualifies for the credits.

While the American Opportunity Tax Credit is basically for those working toward their undergraduate degree, the Lifetime Learning Credit is available for any years of post-secondary education, not just the first four. In addition, with the Lifetime Learning Credit you don't have to be working toward a degree to be eligible.

The Lifetime Learning Credit amount is lower than the American Opportunity Tax Credit, with a maximum credit of **$2,000 per return** versus a **$2,500 per student** maximum for the AOTC. The income thresholds are also lower for the Lifetime Learning Credit before the credit is phased out. The credit is phased out between $53,000 and $63,000 for single, married filing separate, and qualifying widow(er) s; and between $107,000 and $127,000 for those filing married filing jointly.

According to IRS figures, 12 million returns claimed this credit in 2011, with the average credit amount averaging just over $1000.

Qualifying expenses for the Lifetime Learning Credit include tuition and mandatory enrollment fees at an eligible institution. Books and course materials can also count, but only if you are required to purchase them directly from the school. Other expenses, like optional fees and room and board, do not qualify.

6. STUDENT LOAN INTEREST

You can also deduct the interest you pay on a qualified student loan. With this deduction you can claim it as an adjustment to income and you don't have to itemize your deductions. This means you can claim the student loan interest deduction in addition to your standard deduction. Don't miss out on taking advantage of this deduction thinking you have to itemize your deductions to be eligible.

Both undergraduates and graduate students are eligible to deduct the interest expense on their student loan debt. However, you must have been at least a half-time student in a degree program to qualify for this deduction. The following expenses are allowed to be paid with your eligible student loan; books, supplies, room & board, transportation, and other necessary expenses.

Generally, the amount of interest you are allowed to deduct is the lower of $2,500, or the actual amount of student loan interest paid. For 2011, 10 million taxpayers claimed this deduction, with average deduction amount being $967. While the amount of this deduction is close to the average credit amounts for the American Opportunity Credit and the Lifetime Learning credit, remember that each dollar of credit saves you a dollar in taxes, while a deduction only saves you 25 percent of the amount, if you are in the 25 percent tax bracket. So this deduction would save about $242 in taxes.

Like the other tax benefits for education expenses, the student loan interest deduction is phased out at certain income levels. For 2014 the phase out for single taxpayers is from $60,000 to $75,000 and for married filing jointly, the phase-out is from $125,000 to $155,000.

Remember: *You generally cannot claim more than one tax benefit for the same education expense in any one year*

7. TUITION AND FEES DEDUCTION

Another education deduction is the deduction for tuition and fees. You can claim up to $4,000 with this deduction for both undergraduate and graduate education. As with the other education benefits the tuition and fees deduction is also phased out at certain income levels. For 2014 the phase-out is from $60,000 to $80,000 for single, and $130,000 to $160,000 for married filing jointly. And, as with the other education related benefits, you can't file married filing separate and claim this deduction.

The tuition and fees deduction is based on qualified education expenses you pay for yourself, your spouse, or a dependent for whom you claim an exemption on your tax return. For purposes of the tuition and fees deduction, qualified education expenses are tuition and certain related expenses required for enrollment or attendance at an eligible educational institution. Student-activity fees and expenses for course-related books, supplies, and equipment are included in qualified education expenses only if the fees and expenses must be paid to the institution as a condition of enrollment or attendance.

The tuition and fees deduction is also claimed as an adjustment to income, meaning you don't have to itemize your deductions to claim it. This deduction is not as popular as the other education related tax benefits, as only 1.9 million taxpayers claimed this deduction in 2011, however for those who did claim it, the average deduction amount was over $2,200.

Let's look at a few examples to help you in determining what is a qualifying expense.

Let's assume you are a sophomore in your University's degree program in dentistry. This year, in addition to tuition, you are required to pay a fee to the university for the rental of the dental equipment you will use in this program. Because the equipment rental fee must be paid to your University for enrollment and attendance, your equipment rental fee is a qualified education expense.

This time let's assume that you and your friend Susan, are both first-year students at your College, and are required to have certain books and other reading materials to use in your mandatory first-year classes. The college has no policy about how students should obtain these materials, but any student who purchases them from your College's bookstore will receive a bill directly from the college. You bought your books from a friend, so what you paid for them is not a qualified education expense. Susan bought hers at your College's bookstore. Although Susan paid your College directly for her first-year books and materials, her payment is not a qualified education expense either, because the books and materials are not required to be purchased from your College for enrollment or attendance at the institution.

One final example; when you enrolled at College for your freshman year, you had to pay a separate student activity fee in addition to your tuition. This activity fee is required of all students, and is used solely to fund on-campus organizations and activities run by students, such as the student newspaper and the student government. No portion of the fee covers personal expenses. Although labeled as a student activity fee, the fee is required for your enrollment and attendance. Therefore, it is a qualified expense.

8. WORK RELATED EDUCATION

This deduction is for education expenses that are either required by your employer, or are required by law to keep your current job or salary. Examples would include a class that your employer requires you to take, but that you pay for. Another example would be continuing education classes for a CPA, Nurse, Lawyer, or any other profession that has continuing education requirements to maintain their license. For example, CPAs in West Virginia and Virginia are required to have 40 hours of CPE credit each year.

The allowed expenses would include the actual costs of the classes including any books or study materials, plus any transportation or travel expenses, and any other necessary expenses. If you drive your own car to and from class, and use the standard mileage rate, the rate you would use is 56 cents per mile in 2014.

I want to caution you that this deduction is not allowed for meeting the required minimum education requirements for a new job. So taking a course to study for the CPA exam would not count, while continuing education courses would be allowed.

Let me give you a few examples to help clarify.

Assume you are a teacher who has satisfied the minimum requirements for teaching. Your employer requires you to take an additional college course each year to keep your teaching job. If the courses will not qualify you for a new trade or business, they are qualifying work-related education even if you eventually receive a master's degree and an increase in salary because of this extra education.

Now let's assume you repair televisions, radios, and stereo systems for ABC Electronics. To keep up with the latest changes, you take special courses in radio and stereo service. These courses maintain and improve skills required in your work. These would be considered work-related education, unless it also qualifies you for a new trade or business.

Assume you are a full-time engineering student. Although you have not received your degree or certification, you work part time as an engineer for a firm that will employ you as a full-time engineer after you finish college. Although your college engineering courses improve your skills in your present job, they are also needed to meet the minimum job requirements for a full-time engineer. The education is not qualifying work-related education.

One final example, assume you are an accountant and you have met the minimum educational requirements of your employer. Your employer later changes the minimum educational requirements and requires you to take college courses to keep your job. These additional courses can be qualifying work-related education because you have already satisfied the minimum requirements that were in effect when you were hired.

9. CHILD CARE CREDIT

The child-care tax credit can be worth up to 35 percent of your qualifying expenses, depending on your adjusted gross income. According to the IRS, 6.3 million taxpayers claimed this credit in 2011, with an average credit amount of $541.

The child-care credit rules are structured to make the credit available only in situations where the child care is needed in order to help the parents work or look for work. For joint filers, both parents must have earned income from wages, salaries or other compensation, including self-employment income. Full-time students are also treated as having earned income for this purpose..

In addition, the child care has to be directly connected to allowing you to work, it can't be for off-hours babysitting for personal reasons. While this requirement might seem straightforward, there are some nuances to be aware of. Let me give a couple of example to help clarify this requirement.

You and your spouse both work full-time and need some time to relax. The cost of a babysitter while you and your spouse go out to eat is not normally considered a work-related expense. So these costs would not be included in your child-care expenses when computing your credit amount.

Now let's say, that you work during the day, and your spouse works at night and sleeps during the day. You pay for care of your 3-year-old child during the day time hours when you are working and your spouse is sleeping. This child-care expenses would be considered work-related and they would be included for computing your credit amount.

Expenses for a child in nursery school, preschool, or similar programs for children below the level of kindergarten are considered expenses for care.

Expenses to attend kindergarten or a higher grade are not considered expenses for care. Do not use these expenses to figure your credit. However, expenses for before- or after-school care of a child in kindergarten or a higher grade may be expenses for care.

In most cases, children have to be 12 or younger to qualify for the credit. The total expenses that are used to calculate the credit are capped at $3,000 per child and $6,000 for two or more children. Like many other tax credits, the actual amount of credit you can claim is based on your adjust gross income.

Calculating the credit requires taking your actual expenses or the maximum limit, whichever is less. For those with taxpayers with incomes of $15,000 or less, the credit is 35 percent of the child-care expenses, which comes out to a maximum of $1,050 for those with one qualifying child or $2,100 for those with two or more qualifying children. Above $15,000 in income, the credit drops by 1 percentage point for every $2,000 of extra income, hitting a minimum of 20 percent for those taxpayers who earn $43,000 or more in adjusted gross income.

Let's look at an example. A taxpayer with one child has $5,000 in child-care expenses, and an adjusted gross income of $50,000. The calculation would look like this. They would only get to count the $3,000 maximum expense amount, not the $5,000 in actual expenses. The $3,000 would be multiplied by the 20 percent minimum, because their adjusted gross income was higher than $43,000. So the credit would be $600 ($3,000 x 20%).

In addition, if you get partial reimbursement of expenses from a state agency or other source, then you're not entitled to take the credit on the reimbursed amount. Instead, you have to deduct the reimbursement and calculate the credit based on the net amount that you paid.

10. CHILD CARE CREDIT – PART-TIME WORKERS

The same Child-Care Tax Credit that I discussed in the last section is also available for those who work part-time. Of course there are special rules that apply. If you work part-time, you generally must figure your expenses for each day. However, if you have to pay for child-care weekly, monthly, or in another way that includes both days worked and days not worked, you can figure your credit including the expenses you paid for days you did not work. Any day when you work at least 1 hour is considered a day of work for this purpose.

Let's look at a couple of examples. Assume that you work 3 days a week. While you work, your 4-year-old child attends a day care center. The day-care center's care options say that you can pay the center $150 for any 3 days a week or $250 for 5 days a week. Your child attends the center 5 days a week. Your work-related child-care expenses are limited to $150 a week. The two days you are not working do not count as expanses that qualify.

This time let's assume that everything is the same as in the last example, except that the day care center does not offer the three day per week option. In this case the entire $250 weekly fee may be a work-related expenses and would be included in your credit calculation.

11. CHILD CARE CREDIT FOR STUDENTS

The general rule for claiming the child-care tax credit is that the child-care expense must be incurred because you are working. However, the credit is also available for some students. The requirements are that you must be a full-time student. You are a considered a full-time student if you are enrolled at a school for the number of hours or classes that the school considers to be full time. You must have been a full-time student for some part of each of five calendar months during the year. The five months do not have to be consecutive.

The term "school" includes high schools, colleges, universities, and technical, trade, and mechanical schools. A school does not include an on-the-job training course, correspondence school, or a school offering courses only through the Internet.

12. CHILD CARE CREDIT FOR CAMPS

Most working parents are well aware they get a tax break to help cover the costs of sending their child to day care. But most parents overlook the tax advantage of summer day camp costs. During school vacations, many parents turn to these supervised programs to provide child care while they work. Even if it is a specialized camp focusing on soccer, baseball, computers, or art the expenses qualify as child-care. Whether your childcare provider is a sitter at your home or a daycare facility outside the home, you'll get some tax benefit if you qualify for the credit.

One important exception is that overnight camps don't qualify, but the IRS says day camp expenses do qualify for this popular credit.

13. CHILD AND DEPENDENT CARE CREDIT

In the previous sections I have called this the child-care credit because that is the most common use of this credit. But it is actually the Child and Dependent Care Credit. In addition to children under age 13, others that qualify for the credit are a spouse that is physically or mentally unable to care for themselves and who live with you, or another dependent you lives with you for over half of the year and is unable to care for themselves.

A person who cannot dress, clean, or feed themselves because of physical or mental problems are considered not able to care for themselves. Also, anyone who must have constant attention to prevent them from injuring themselves or others are considered not able to care for themselves.

14. CHILD TAX CREDIT

You can claim up to $1,000 per qualifying child. A qualifying child is your son, daughter, stepchild, foster child, bother, sister, or a descendant of any of them, for example, a grandchild, niece or nephew. The child also has to be under age 17 at the end of the year, can't have provided more than half of their own support, and must have lived with you for than half of the year and are a US citizen.

There are a couple of limitations with the Child Tax Credit, one it is not refundable, in that, the amount of the credit can't be more than the amount of tax that you owe. There is also an income limitation, for single taxpayers the limit is an modified adjust gross income (MAGI) of $75,000, $110,000 for married-filing jointly, and $55,000 for married filing separate.

Your tax credit is reduced by $50 for every $1,000 that your MAGI exceeds the amounts listed above.

For 2011, 23.1 million taxpayers claimed this credit, with an average credit amount of $1215. Remember, the limit, is $1,000 per child.

15. EXCESS SOCIAL SECURITY AND RRTA TAX WITHHELD

You probably know that the amount of your income subject to Social Security taxes is limited. For 2014 the maximum amount of taxable earnings is $117,000. If you only had one job during the year, you shouldn't have a problem. Your payroll department should just stop withholding the Social Security taxes once you reach this threshold.

However, if you had more than one employer during the year, either through working two jobs at once or by switching jobs during the year. Then you should have had excess Social Security taxes withheld from your paycheck. When you have more than one job in a year, each of your employers are required to withhold Social Security taxes from your wages without regard to what the other employers may have withheld. With this being the case, if your total income for the year exceeds the threshold, you may end up with total Social Security taxes being withheld that exceeds the maximum.

For example, let's say in 2014 you worked at XYZ Company and earned $50,000 before changing jobs and going to work for ABC Company. The ABC Company you earned $75,000. You would have had Social Security taxes withheld from all $125,000 that you earned in 2014, but the maximum income subject to Social Security taxes for 2014 is only $117,000. You can claim a refund for the Social Security taxes withheld from the last $8,000 earnings. The credit for overpayments is claimed on Line 69 of your 1040.

16. RETIREMENT SAVINGS CONTRIBUTIONS CREDIT

The Retirement Savings Contributions Credit is contributions that you make to certain eligible retirement plans, or individual retirement arrangement (IRA). Your credit rate is based on your adjusted gross income and can be as high as 50 percent or as low as 10 percent. Obviously, the lower your income, the higher the credit rate. Your credit rate also depends on your filing status. Your income and filing status when taken together will determine the maximum credit you are allowed to take. There is also a cap on the maximum adjusted gross income to be eligible for the credit. In addition, dependents and full-time students are not allowed to take this credit.

The following types of contributions are eligible for the credit; contributions to a traditional or Roth IRS; or salary reduction contributions to; a 401(k); a section 404(b) annuity; a SIMPLE IRS plan; a salary reduction SEP, and contributions to a section 501(c)(18) plan.

The maximum contribution taken into account is $2,000 per person. On a joint return, up to $2,000 is taken into account for each spouse.

Let's look at an example. If you are married and file a joint return and have an adjusted gross income of $50,000. You would be eligible for a 10% credit. Let's assume you contributed $2,000. Your credit would be $200 (10% of the $2,000).

The credit is non-refundable, but it is in addition to any deduction you may get for your IRA contribution. According to IRS figures, in 2011, 6.4 million taxpayers claimed this credit, with an average credit amount of about $175.

17. TAX DEDUCTION FOR TRADITIONAL IRA CONTRIBUTION

In addition to the tax credit that I discussed in the previous section, your contributions to a traditional IRA may also allow you to take a tax deduction, and any earnings are tax-deferred or tax-free. For the average taxpayer, this is one of the largest deductions. In 2011, a little over 2.5 million taxpayers claimed this deduction, with the average deduction amount totaling over $4,300.

For 2014 the maximum that you can contribute to your traditional IRS is the smaller of $5,500, $6,500 if you are age 50 or older, or your taxable compensation for the year.

Let's look at a couple of examples.

Jim, who is 40 years old and single, earns $27,000 in 2014. His IRA contributions for 2014 are limited to $5,500.

Sam, an unmarried college student working part-time, earns $3,000 in 2014. His IRA contributions for 2014 are limited to $3,000, the amount of his compensation.

Sally, is 60 years old and single, earns $40,000 in 2014. Her IRA contributions for 2014 can be up to $6,500. Sally can contribute an extra $1,000 because she is age 50 or older.

18. CONTRIBUTE TO AN IRA EVEN IF COVERED BY ANOTHER RETIREMENT PLAN

Many people think that they can't contribute to an IRA if they are covered by another retirement plan through their employer. That is not the case. You can contribute to a traditional or Roth IRA whether or not you participate in another retirement plan through your employer or business. However, you might not be able to deduct 100% of your traditional IRA contributions if you or your spouse participates in another retirement plan at work, and your Roth IRA contributions might be limited if your income exceeds a certain level.

You are considered to be covered by an employer retirement plan for a tax year if your employer (or your spouse's employer) has a:

- Defined contribution plan (profit-sharing, 401(k), stock bonus and money purchase pension plan) and any contributions or forfeitures were allocated to your account for the plan year ending with or within the tax year;

- IRA-based plan (SEP, SARSEP or SIMPLE IRA plan) and you had an amount contributed to your IRA for the plan year that ends with or within the tax year; or

- Defined benefit plan (pension plan that pays a retirement benefit spelled out in the plan) and you are eligible to participate for the plan year ending with or within the tax year.

For 2014 the Adjusted Gross Income limit is $60,000 for single taxpayers and those filing as head of household, $96,000 for those filing as married filing jointly, and $10,000 for married filing separate. If your income is below those respective levels, then your contributions are fully deductible. The deduction is phased out between $60,000 and $70,000 for single and head of household filers, and between $96,000 and $116,000 for married filing jointly. If your AGI is above the phase out ranges of above $10,000 if married filing separate, then the contributions are not deductible.

19. HOME MORTGAGE INTEREST – NOT JUST FIRST MORTGAGE

Pretty much everyone knows that home mortgage interest is deductible. For most taxpayers, home mortgage interest is the single largest itemized deduction. According to IRS data, in 2011, 35.5 million taxpayers claimed the home mortgage interest deduction, if you recall only, about 46.5 million taxpayers choose to itemize their deductions. Based on these figures, about 76 percent of all taxpayers who itemize, claim the home mortgage interest deduction, with the average deduction amount being just over $10,000.

I want to give you some tips to insure you get the largest deduction possible.

It's not just interest on your first mortgage that you get to deduct. For tax purposes a home mortgage is considered to be any loan that is secured by your main home or a second home. It includes your primary mortgage as well as any second mortgages, home equity loans, and refinanced mortgages.

20. HOME MORTGAGE INTEREST – FINANCING CAR PURCHASE

Let me give you an example of how you can use this information to your advantage. Let's assume you want to buy a new car and you need to finance $20,000 of the purchase price. One option would be to get a car loan from your local bank. At the time of writing, an average interest rate on a new car loan is about 3% and none of the interest would be deductible.

As an alternative, you can use a home equity loan to finance the purchase of the car. The interest rate on a home equity loan at the present time is about the same 3% rate. So the amount of interest paid would be the same for both loan types, but you would get to deduct the interest if you used a home equity loan. Assuming a 25% tax bracket, this would save you about $150 in taxes in the first year. There would be additional amounts saved in later years of the loan. Each year the tax savings would get smaller as the amount of interest is reduced.

However, I don't want you to get so fixated on the tax savings that you miss the bigger picture. That is, what is going to result in more money in your pocket! There is one situation when you may not want to use the home equity loan to finance a car purchase. Car makers will sometimes run promotions with very low interest rates, sometimes even interest free. With a very low interest rate loan from the car dealership, you would need to compute whether the tax savings from using the home equity loan would offset the lower interest rate from the dealership. Let's say the dealership offers 2.5% financing. You would pay about $500 in interest the first year, with no tax savings. With the home equity loan, you would pay $600 in interest in the first year, but you would then save $150 in taxes. This would result in a net of $450 out of pocket for the interest expense. The home equity loan would still be slightly better than the car dealership financing at a slightly lower rate. But if the car dealer offers 2.0% financing, then the interest paid would total $400. This is less than the out-of-pocket costs of using a home equity loan. The point is, that you would just need to compare. In my examples I used a 25% tax bracket; of course you would use the actual bracket you are in. The higher your tax rate, the more likely it is that the home equity loan is going to be the best option.

However, if you can get interest free financing, then you're not paying any interest at all. That is obviously better than paying $600 in interest with the home equity loan, and then saving $150 on your taxes. You would be $450 better off with the no interest car loan.

21. HOME MORTGAGE INTEREST – PAY OFF CREDIT CARD DEBT

Another potential way to increase your tax savings is if you carry a balance on your high interest rate credit card, you can use a home equity loan to pay off the credit card debt. Credit cards usually have high interest rates, 18% is not unusual and the interest paid is not tax deductible. Let's assume a $20,000 balance and an 18% interest rate. If the balance remains on the credit card, you would pay $3,600 per year in interest with no tax deduction.

If the credit card balance is paid off with a home equity loan charging a 3% interest rate. The interest expense would be $600, which would be deductible. This would result in $150 of tax savings if you are in the 25% tax bracket. So your net, out-of-pocket expense would be $450 for the home equity loan. This is $3,150 less than the interest expense on the credit card.

22. HOME MORTGAGE INTEREST – NOT JUST FOR HOUSES

What qualifies as a home may also surprise you. It's not just houses and condos that qualify as a home. The IRS says a home can be a house, condominium, cooperative, mobile home, boat, or similar property.

However, I don't want to you to think that your bass boat can be called your home. To qualify as a home, the "home" must provide basic living accommodations, including sleeping space, a toilet, and cooking facilities.

So, with that said, if you have a boat that meets the three criteria; of a place to sleep, a toilet, and a kitchen. Your boat would qualify as your home or second home and the interest paid would be tax deductible. The same goes for an RV or camper. You don't even need to use it during the year, if it is a second "home", as long as you don't rent it out to others.

23. MEDICAL AND DENTAL EXPENSES

Medical and dental expenses are deductible once they exceed 10 percent of adjusted gross income, or 7.5 percent of AGI if either you or your spouse are 65 or older. The 10 percent of AGI threshold is new, until the passage of the Affordable Care Act the threshold was 7.5 percent of AGI for all taxpayers, not just those 65 or older.

This is another significant deduction for those taxpayers who itemize. In 2011, 10.4 million taxpayers claimed this deduction, with total medical expenses averaging over $12,400. Due to the income limitation, which was 7.5 percent of AGI at the time, a little over $8,100 of the $12,400 was deductible.

An important note is that you can't deduct expenses that are reimbursed or paid by someone else. So if your health insurance company either pays your health care bill or reimburses you later, those expenses are not deductible.

In order to claim the medical or dental expense deduction, you have to itemize your deductions. The expenses can be for you, your spouse, or dependents.

Some of the more obvious expenses that can be included here

include; doctors' visits, prescription drugs, hospital stays, medically necessary surgeries, etc., there are far too many to list them all here. I do want to cover some of the expenses that you may not think to include in medical and dental expenses.

24. MEDICAL AND DENTAL EXPENSES – TRANSPORTATION/TRAVEL

You can include in medical expenses amounts you paid for transportation primarily for, and essential to, medical care. This can include bus, taxi, train, or plane fares or ambulance service, transportation expenses of a parent who must go with a child who needs medical care; transportation expenses of a nurse or other person who can give injections, medications, or other treatment required by a patient who is traveling to get medical care and is unable to travel alone, and Transportation expenses for regular visits to see a mentally ill dependent, if these visits are recommended as a part of treatment.

You can also include any out-of-pocket expenses, such as the cost of gas and oil, when you use a car for medical reasons. However, you cannot include depreciation, insurance, general repair, or maintenance expenses.

If you do not want to use your actual expenses for 2014, you can use the standard medical mileage rate of 23.5 cents per mile.

You can also include parking fees and tolls. You can add these fees and tolls to your medical expenses whether you use your actual expenses or the standard mileage rate.

Let me give you an example. In 2014, Jim drove 3,000 miles for medical reasons. He spent $550 for gas, $30 for oil, and $100 for tolls and parking. He wants to figure the amount he can include in medical expenses both ways to see which gives him the greater deduction.

He figures the actual expenses first. He adds the $550 for gas, the $30 for oil, and the $100 for tolls and parking for a total of $680.

He then figures the standard mileage amount. He multiplies 3,000 by 23.5 cents a mile for a total of $705. He then adds the $100 tolls and parking for a total of $805.

Jim includes the $805 of car expenses with his other medical expenses for the year because the $805 is more than the $680 he figured using his actual expenses.

You can also include in medical expenses amounts you pay for transportation to another city if the trip is primarily for, and essential to, receiving medical services. You may be able to include up to $50 for each night for each person. You can include lodging for a person traveling with the person receiving the medical care. For example, if a parent is traveling with a sick child, up to $100 per night can be included as a medical expense for lodging. However, meals can't be included.

25. MEDICAL AND DENTAL EXPENSES – WEIGHT LOSS

This is another one of those expenses that many people miss when totaling their medical and dental expenses for the year. But, as always there are limitations as to who qualifies. You can include in medical expenses amounts you pay to lose weight if it is a treatment for a specific disease diagnosed by a physician (such as obesity, hypertension, or heart disease). You must have the doctor's orders in writing.

Amounts that you can deduct includes fees you pay for membership in a weight reduction group, which can be at a commercial program like Jenny Craig or Weight Watchers, or it can be with a physician or hospital-based weight-loss program, as well as fees for attendance at periodic meetings. You can also deduct the costs of behavioral counseling, appointments with physicians, dieticians, and nutritionists.

You cannot include membership dues in a gym, health club, or spa as medical expenses, but you can include separate fees charged there for weight loss activities. You also can't deduct the cost of diet food, which is considered a personal expense, or the costs of home exercise equipment.

26. MEDICAL AND DENTAL EXPENSES – MEDICAL INSURANCE PREMIUMS

You can include in medical expenses insurance premiums you pay for policies that cover medical care. Medical care policies can provide payment for treatment that includes: hospitalization, surgical services, X-rays, Prescription drugs and insulin, dental care, replacement of lost or damaged contact lenses.

However, you can't deduct premiums you paid with "pre-tax" dollars. Pre-tax means you already received a tax benefit by not paying taxes on it, so you can't get a second benefit on the same dollars.

Generally, you can also deduct the premiums you pay for Medicare B (supplemental medical insurance) and Medicare D (voluntary prescription drug insurance program.)

But, if you are covered under social security (or if you are a government employee who paid Medicare tax), the amount paid for Medicare A is not deductible.

27. MEDICAL AND DENTAL EXPENSES – LONG TERM CARE INSURANCE

A portion of any premiums you pay for long-term care insurance may be included in your medical and dental expenses total. The amount varies from a low of $370 for a person age 40 and under, up to $4,660 for someone age 71 and older. These limits are per person, so if married filing jointly each spouse could include the appropriate amount based on their age.

The deductible amounts by age are as follows, for those under age 40 the deductible limit is $370, for 40 to 49 it's $700, 50 to 59 $1,400, 60 to 69 $3,720, and 70 and over $4,660.

Tax Savings Tip: Long-term care insurance premiums may be paid from a Health Savings Account (HSA) up to the limits shown above.

A self-employed individual can deduct 100% of his/her out-of-pocket long-term care insurance premiums, up to the Eligible Premium amounts. The portion of premiums that exceeds the Eligible Premium amount is not deductible as a medical expense. The deductible amount includes eligible premiums paid for spouses and dependents. It is not necessary to meet the 10.0% AGI threshold in order to take this deduction.

28. MEDICAL AND DENTAL EXPENSES – CAPITAL EXPENDITURES

You can include in medical expenses amounts you pay for special equipment to be installed in your home, or for improvements, if their main purpose is medical care for you, your spouse, or your dependent. The cost of permanent improvements that increase the value of your property may be partly included as a medical expense. In these cases the cost of the improvement is reduced by the increase in the value of your property. The difference is a medical expense. If the value of your property is not increased by the improvement, the entire cost is included as a medical expense.

Certain improvements made to accommodate a home to your disabled condition, or that of your spouse or your dependents who live with you, do not usually increase the value of the home and the cost can be included in full as medical expenses. These improvements include, but are not limited to, the following items.

- Constructing entrance or exit ramps for your home.
- Widening doorways at entrances or exits to your home.

- Widening or otherwise modifying hallways and interior doorways.
- Installing railings, support bars, or other modifications to bathrooms.
- Lowering or modifying kitchen cabinets and equipment.
- Moving or modifying electrical outlets and fixtures.
- Installing porch lifts and other forms of lifts (but elevators generally add value to the house).
- Modifying fire alarms, smoke detectors, and other warning systems.
- Modifying stairways.
- Adding handrails or grab bars anywhere (whether or not in bathrooms).
- Modifying hardware on doors.
- Modifying areas in front of entrance and exit doorways.
- Grading the ground to provide access to the residence.

These capital costs can be a major expense and can offer a substantial tax savings, however, only reasonable costs to accommodate a home to a disabled condition are considered medical care. Any additional costs for personal motives, such as for architectural or aesthetic reasons, are not medical expenses, and can't be included here.

29. HEALTH INSURANCE PREMIUM TAX CREDIT

Beginning in 2014, taxpayers who purchase health insurance through an Exchange are eligible for this tax credit.

The Health Insurance Premium Tax Credit will help reduce the premium costs for low to middle income Americans. Households with incomes between 100% and 400% of the Federal Poverty Level who purchase coverage through a health insurance exchange are eligible for this tax credit.

The amount of the credit is based on the premium for the second lowest cost "silver plan" and varies with income. In addition, the credit will be both refundable and advanceable. Meaning that you can receive it even if you have no tax liability, and you can choose to receive it at the time you purchase the insurance instead of waiting to be reimbursed after filing your tax return.

30. STATE AND LOCAL INCOME TAXES

If you itemize deductions you can elect to deduct any state and local income taxes you paid or you can choose to deduct the state and local sales taxes you paid. You can't deduct both. First I'll cover state and local income taxes.

Since most states have an income tax, this is another common itemized deduction. In 2011, 33.7 million taxpayers claimed this deduction, with the average deduction amount being over $7,800. I want to point out that the averages I'm providing are based on just the taxpayers who claim that particular deduction or credit; it is not based on all tax returns filed.

This deduction seems straightforward, but like many tax issues it is a little more complicated than it would seem at first glance.

Let's look at what income taxes you can include here. You can include any state and local income taxes withheld from your salary in that year. Most people get that part, what many taxpayers miss are the other taxes that can be included here. You can also deduct state and local income taxes for a prior year which were paid in the current year. Such as taxes you paid for last year's taxes when you filed your tax return in the spring. However, you can't deduct any penalties or interest.

In additional you can include any state and local estimated tax payments that you made during the year, including any part of a prior year refund that you chose to have credited to this year's state or local income taxes.

Also, you do not have to reduce your deduction by any refund or credit you expect to receive for the current year or that you actually received this year for an earlier year.

31. STATE AND LOCAL SALES TAXES

As I mentioned earlier, you can choose to deduct your state and local sales taxes paid instead of income taxes paid. If you choose to deduct your sales taxes paid, you can deduct your actual expenses, or you can use the optional sales tax tables that the IRS publishes. As I mentioned in the last section, 33.7 million taxpayers deducted income taxes, an additional 10.8 million deducted sales taxes paid in 2011. The average deduction for sales taxes paid was a little over $1,400.

Generally, you can choose to deduct your actual state and local sales taxes paid if the tax rate was the same as the general sales tax rate. However, you can deduct the sales tax on food, clothing, medical supplies, and motor vehicles even if the tax rate was less than the general tax rate.

If you paid sales tax on a car at a higher rate than the general sales tax rate, then you can only deduct the amount of tax you would have paid using the general sales tax rate.

If you received a refund of sales taxes this year for sales taxes paid this year, then reduce your deduction by that amount. However, if you received a refund of sales taxes this year for taxes paid in prior years, you don't have to reduce your deduction.

Alternatively, you can choose to use the IRS tables or the Sales Tax Deduction Calculator on the IRS website at www.irs.gov/Individuals/Sales-Tax-Deduction-Calculator.

32. REAL ESTATE TAXES

If you are a homeowner you can deduct real estate taxes you paid on real estate that you own that was not used for business. You are able to take this deduction whether you pay the taxes directly yourself, or if they are included in your mortgage payment. If they are included in your mortgage payment you can only deduct the actual amount the mortgage company paid to the taxing authority.

This is another significant deduction for a large percentage of taxpayers who itemize. In 2011, 40.1 million taxpayers claimed the real estate tax deduction, with the average deduction totaling over $4,300.

There are some exclusions to this deduction, these include any charges included in your real estate taxes for improvements that will tend to increase the value of your property. An example would be an assessment to build a new sidewalk. However, a charge is deductible if is only used to maintain an existing public facility. For example, a charge to repair an existing sidewalk. Another example, is an assessment for the repair and resurfacing of streets is a deductible tax. However, an assessment levied for the lengthening or widening of the streets is not.

33. PERSONAL PROPRTY TAXES

This seems like a very straight-forward deduction. If you look at your records you can see exactly the amount you paid in personal property tax, however, all of it may not be deductible.

Your personal property taxes are deductible as long as the taxes were based on the value alone and were imposed on a yearly basis.

For example, if you pay a yearly registration fee for your car and part of the fee is based on the value of the car and part of the fee is based on the weight of the car. You can only deduct the part of the fee that is based on the value.

In 2011, about half as many taxpayers claimed the personal property tax deduction as claimed the real estate tax deduction, with 19.9 million taxpayer claiming the personal property tax deduction. The average deduction amount was a little of $400.

34. PET EXPENSES

Yes, it's true, in some cases pet expenses are deductible. With the cost of pet food and veterinary care these days, this can amount to a significant tax deduction if your pet qualifies. There are two main categories of deductible pet expenses. The first is if you have a medical condition that can be helped by a service animal, then all of your medical expenses above 10% of your adjusted gross income are deductible, including your pet expanses.

The other category is if your pet qualifies as a business expense. Examples of this may be if you own a feed supply store and your cats provide a vital service to protect the feed from mice and rats. Another example is a junkyard owner who uses guard dogs. Then all of the pet expenses including food and vet bills would be a deductible business expense.

I don't have exact number from the IRS as to how many people get to claim pet related deductions, as they would be included in the total medical expenses or business expenses. I'm sure the percentage of taxpayers who are able to qualify is small, I just wanted to point out the fact that the deduction is available to those who do qualify.

35. MOVING EXPENSES

If you moved due to a change in your job or business location you may be able to deduct your reasonable moving expenses. To qualify your move has to be closely related to the start of work in the new job. What this means in practical terms is that if you moved within one year of the date that you first worked in the new location.

In addition, your new workplace has to be at least 50 miles further from your old home than your old job was from your old home and the distance from your new home to the new job location is not more than the distance from your former home to the new job location. Plus you need to work full-time for at least 39 weeks in the first 12 months after your move.

However if you are relocating to the United States from another country as a retiree, you can deduct your moving costs without needing to start a new job in the USA. In other words, retirees from abroad do not need to meet the time test.

Because of the restrictions related to what moves qualify, only about 1 million taxpayers were able to claim this deduction in 2011. However, for those who meet the requirements, the deduction can be substantial, with an average deduction of over $2,900.

The moving expenses that you can deduct include the costs of moving your household goods and personal effects and your traveling expenses, which includes lodging expenses, but not meals.

If you travel by car you can track your actual expenses, such as the amount you actually pay for gas and oil for your car. If you use this method you have to keep your receipts. Or you can use the standard mileage rate of 23.5 cents per mile. No matter which method you use, you can deduct any parking fees and tolls. But, you can't deduct general repairs, maintenance, insurance, or depreciation on your car.

You can also deduct the costs of packing, crating, and transporting your household goods and personal effects. As well as the costs of shipping your car or your pets to your new home, this can also be deducted.

Not all moves qualify for this deduction, but if your move qualifies, this can be a significant deduction.

36. CHARITABLE CONTRIBUTIONS

It's hard to overlook the larger contributions you made during the year, either by check or through payroll deduction. You have a record of these, all you need to do is look at your bank records or a December pay stub to see these amounts. But not all of your charitable gifts are so easy to account for or to remember.

Contributions can be in cash, property, or out-of-pocket expenses you paid to do volunteer work. In order for your contribution to be deductible, the organization that you gave to must be considered a qualified charitable organization. Examples include: churches, synagogues, Boy Scouts, Red Cross, United Way, Fraternal Order, Non-profit hospitals, etc.

If you want to check to see if an organization is eligible to receive tax-deductible contributions, you can check with the organization directly, or the IRS has an online search tool at: http://www.irs.gov/Charities-&-Non-Profits/Exempt-Organizations-Select-Check

37. LARGE CONTRIBUTIONS

For donations of $250 or more you have to have a contemporaneous statement from the charity which shows the amount that you donated and whether the charity provided you with any goods or services in exchange for your donation.

To be contemporaneous, you have to obtain the written acknowledgment no later than the date you file your tax return for the year the contribution is made. The written acknowledgment from the charity must state whether the charity provided any goods or services in consideration for the contribution. If the charity did provide goods or services to you in exchange for the contribution, then the written acknowledgment must include a good faith estimate of the value of the goods or services

When you are figuring whether a gift is $250 or more you don't have to combine separate donations to the same organization. For example, if you give $25 to your church each week, for a total of $1,300 for the year, you would treat each $25 payment as a separate gift. If you made donations through payroll deduction, each deduction is treated as a separate gift.

38. CASH OR CHECK CONTRIBUTIONS

If you make any cash contributions, regardless of the amount, you have to be able to provide a record of the contribution. This can be in the form of a cancelled check or credit card statement, or it can be a written receipt from the charity. The receipt must show the name of the charity, the date, and the amount contributed.

Written records prepared by the taxpayer, such as check registers or personal notations, are no longer sufficient to support charitable contributions. Bank records for this recordkeeping requirement include bank or credit union statements, canceled checks, or credit card statements. They must show the date paid or posted, the name of the charity, and the amount of the payment.

According to IRS records, 34.5 million taxpayers who itemized in 2011 claimed the deduction for contributions to charity in the form of cash or checks. The average deduction amount totaled just over $4,000.

39. NON-CASH OR CHECK CONTRIBUTIONS

If you made a contribution of used items like clothing or furniture, you can deduct the fair market value of the item at the time you gave them. The fair market value is what a willing buyer would pay a willing seller for the item.

If the amount of your deduction is more than $500 you will have to complete Form 8283. If the donation was a motor vehicle, boat, or airplane, you also will need to attach a statement from the charity.

If you give property to a charity you should keep a receipt of statement from the organization. Your records should also include how you determined the value at the time you gave it.

It is important to note that you can't deduct the value of your time or services you provided to an organization.

While not quite as common as contributions made by cash or check, 22.5 million taxpayers made contributions of another type in 2011, averaging over $1,900.

40. CONTRIBUTIONS WHEN YOU RECEIVED BENEFITS

If you made a gift to a charity and received a benefit in return, such as food, entertainment, or merchandise, you can still take the deduction but only for the amount that is over the value of the item received.

For example, if you paid $100 to a charity to attend a fund-raising dinner, and the value of the dinner was $40, you would be able to deduct $60.

Another example, at a fundraising auction conducted by a charity, you pay $600 for a week's stay at a beach house. The amount you pay is no more than the fair rental value. You have not made a deductible charitable contribution. So you would not be entitled to any deduction.

Athletic events

If you make a payment to, or for the benefit of, a college or university and, as a result, you receive the right to buy tickets to an athletic event in the athletic stadium of the college or university, you can deduct 80% of the payment as a charitable contribution. If any part of your payment is for tickets, rather than the right to buy tickets, that part is not deductible. Subtract the price of the tickets from your payment. You can deduct 80% of the remaining amount as a charitable contribution.

For example, you pay $300 a year for membership in a university's athletic scholarship program. The only benefit of membership is that you have the right to buy one season ticket for a seat in a designated area of the stadium at the university's home football games. You can deduct $240 (80% of $300) as a charitable contribution.

Another example, the facts are the same as in the example above except your $300 payment includes the purchase of one season ticket for the stated ticket price of $120. You must subtract the usual price of a ticket ($120) from your $300 payment. The result is $180. Your deductible charitable contribution is $144 (80% of $180).

Travel

You can also deduct travel expenses, such as airfare and other transport, accommodations, and meals, when performing services away from home. This might include trips to attend a convention or board meeting, or taking underprivileged kids on a camping trip.

However, there are important limitations: You cannot gain significant personal pleasure, recreation, or vacation from the travel. And you must really be working – just going along on an outing while performing minimal duties, or even no duties for significant parts of the trip, won't cut it.

41. VOLUNTEER MILEAGE

When most people think of their charitable contributions most think of cash contributions. But there are many other things that qualify.

If you volunteer for a qualified organization you can deduct the cost of gas and oil directly related to getting to and from the place where you volunteer, or if you use your car to provide a service to the charity, like delivering meals to the elderly. You cannot deduct general repair and maintenance expenses, depreciation, registration fees, or the costs of tires or insurance. Alternatively, you can deduct 14 cents per mile if you don't want to figure your actual costs.

In addition, you can deduct parking fees and tolls whether you use your actual expenses or the standard mileage rate. As always you must keep contemporaneous, reliable written records of your car expenses.

Alternatively, for those volunteers taking public transportation you can deduct the cost of taking the subway, bus, or taxi fare.

42. VOLUNTEER UNIFORM COSTS

Volunteers can also deduct the costs of buying and cleaning their uniforms if the place where they volunteer is a qualify organization, if the uniforms are not suitable for everyday use, and if the uniforms are required to be worn when volunteering.

An example of this would be if you volunteer as a Red Cross nurse's aide at a hospital and were required to wear a particular uniform.

Not only can you deduct the purchase price of your uniform, you can deduct any upkeep costs.

43. MISCELLANEOUS DEDUCTIONS

There are three general categories that these expenses fall into: unreimbursed employee expenses, tax preparation fees, and "other" expenses. The roadblock keeping these deductions from being even more valuable to taxpayers is the requirement that all together, the miscellaneous expenses must total more than 2 percent of adjusted gross income before they are deductable. For example, a taxpayer with an adjusted gross income of $25,000 must have expenses in these areas totaling $500 or more before seeing any tax benefit. Even then, only the amount over the threshold is deductible. So the taxpayer with $25,000 income and $1,200 in tax-allowable miscellaneous expenses would only be able to deduct $700.

In 2011, a total of 28.7 million taxpayers claimed deductions in one or more of the miscellaneous categories; the average dollar amount for those taxpayers was just over $4,200. Of those 28.7 million taxpayers, 11.8 million taxpayers had expenses that exceeded the 2 percent of AGI threshold. Those taxpayers who exceeded the threshold actually got to deduct an average of over $7,300.

While the two percent threshold is tough for many taxpayers to reach, as you can see from the IRS data it's not impossible if you know all of the possible expenses that the IRS considers as allowable miscellaneous deductions. The following sections are going to help you to maximize this deduction for yourself.

44. TAX PREPARATION FEES

You may or may not know that you can deduct the cost of preparing your taxes. According to the IRS Statistics of Income, in 2011, 22.1 million people included their tax preparation fees in their miscellaneous expenses. The average amount of the expense was $315.

What probably will surprise you is all of the items that can be included in this deduction. You can deduct all of the expenses related to preparing and filing your taxes. This includes your tax preparer's fees, any software you purchased to help you prepare your taxes, and even "how-to" books, like this one. Yes, your purchase price of this book is deductible as part of your miscellaneous expenses total. In addition, you can include the cost of making copies of your tax return, paying for return-receipt postage or overnight delivery of your return to the IRS.

If you file electronically, you can deduct the electronic return filing fee, and if you paid by credit card you can even deduct the convenience fee that you were charged.

As you can see, there many expenses in this category that most people wouldn't know to include, even if they knew tax preparation fees were deductible in general terms.

45. UNREIMBURSED EMPLOYEE EXPENSES - GENERAL

You can deduct unreimbursed employee expenses that are for carrying on your trade or business of being and employee as long as they are considered ordinary and necessary. According to the IRS, an expense is ordinary if it is common and accepted in your trade, business, or profession. An expense is necessary if it is appropriate and helpful to your business. It doesn't have to be required to be considered necessary.

For 2011, 14.7 million people claim unreimbursed employee expenses, averaging over $5,200 each. Remember that these deduction are only deductible once over the 2 percent of AGI requirement. So of the 14.7 million taxpayers who had unreimbursed employee expenses, 8.7 million had expenses that exceeded the 2 percent of AGI threshold. Those taxpayers averaged over $6,700 of expenses that were actually deductible.

There are many different types of expenses that can be included as an unreimbursed employee expense. In the following sections I am going to list most of these expenses, for some of them I'll cover them in some detail, for other I won't go into much more detail than to simply list them and provide a basic summary. That is because these expenses are so straight forward, and there simply isn't much to say about them I didn't want to ignore them and not list them at all, so that is the reason some of the following topic sections are so short.

46. BUSINESS LIABILITY INSURANCE

As an employee, if you paid for professional liability insurance to protect you against personal liability, the premium costs are deductible as an unreimbursed employee expense.

Some of the most common professions requiring professional liability insurance would be doctors, attorneys, police, bus drivers, and accountants.

47. DEPRECIATION ON COMPUTERS

You are allowed to claim a depreciation deduction on your computer that you own but use in your work as an employee if you use the computer for the convenience of your employer. This means that your use of the computer is for a substantial business reason of your employer. You must consider all facts in making this determination. Use of your computer during your regular working hours to carry on your employer's business is generally for the convenience of your employer.

It must also be required as a condition of your employment. This means that you can't properly perform your duties without the computer. Whether you can properly perform your duties without it depends on all the facts and circumstances. It is not necessary that your employer explicitly requires you to use your computer. But neither is it enough that your employer merely states that your use of the computer is a condition of your employment.

48. PROFESSIONAL DUES

As an employee you may able to deduct dues you pay to professional organizations, such as medical associations and bar associations, or to the chamber of commerce and other similar organizations, if the membership helps you carry out the duties of your job. Similar organizations include: Boards of trade, business leagues, civic or public service organizations, Real estate boards, and trade associations.

Of course to be deductible, like for all of the unreimbursed employee expenses, you must pay the expense, not your employer.

49. EDUCATOR EXPENSES

If you are an eligible educator, you can deduct $250 of qualified expenses as an adjustment to income, rather than as a miscellaneous itemized deduction. IRS figures show that 3.8 million educators claimed this deduction in 2011, with the average deduction being the maximum of $250. This tells me that most educators are spending more than this out of pocket each year, with the additional amount being included under unreimbursed employee expenses subject to the 2 percent of AGI requirement.

You are considered to be an eligible educator, if you teach kindergarten through grade 12, or if you are a counselor, principal, or aide in the school for at least 900 hours during the school year.

Qualified expenses include ordinary and necessary expenses paid for books, supplies, equipment (including computer equipment, software, and service), and other materials used in the classroom.

I know many teachers who commonly bring supplies to the classroom which were purchased with their own money due to lack of funds from the school. I hope they are not missing this deduction.

As I mentioned above, you can deduct the first $250 in qualified expenses as an adjustment to income. If you spent more than $250, the remainder can be deducted as a miscellaneous itemized deduction subject to the 2 percent limit.

50. JOB SEARCH EXPENSES

If you looked for a new job in your present occupation this year, even if you didn't get a new job you may be able to deduct some of the expenses that you incurred in your job search. Expenses that you can deduct include any fees you paid to an employment or outplacement agency as part of your job search for a new job in your present occupation. You may also deduct the cost of preparing and mailing your resume to prospective employers.

If you travel somewhere, and while you are there, you look for a new job, you may be able to deduct travel costs to and from that location if the reason for the trip was primarily to look for a new job. The amount of time you spent looking for a new job should be compared to the amount of time spent on personal activities to help determine if the trip was primarily to look for a new job.

Even if you can't deduct the travel expenses to and from the location, because the trip wasn't primarily for looking for a new job, you can still deduct the expenses of looking for a new job while you are in that area. You can use the standard mileage rate of 56 cents per mile.

Although job-hunting expenses are not deductible when looking for your first job, moving expenses to get to that job are. And you get this write-off even if you don't itemize.

To qualify for the deduction, your first job must be at least 50 miles away from your old home. If you do qualify, you can deduct the cost of getting yourself and your household goods to the new area. If you drove your own car, you can deduct 23.5 cents a mile in 2014, plus what you paid for parking and tolls.

51. LEGAL FEES

If you incur any legal fees related to doing or keeping your job those fees are deductible as an unreimbursed employee expense under the miscellaneous itemized expense deduction.

In order to be deductible as a trade or business expense while acting as an employee, an expenditure must be both ordinary and necessary.

Legal expenses that otherwise qualify for deduction are deductible only as long as they are also reasonable in amount.

For example, assume you are a bus driver and are in an accident. A passenger on the bus is injured. They sue both the bus company and you as an individual. Any legal fees you incur to defend yourself in the lawsuit would be deductible as an unreimbursed employee expense.

52. LICENSES AND REGULATORY FEES

You can deduct the amount you pay each year to state or local governments for licenses and regulatory fees for your trade, business, or profession.

Examples of these would include fees Medical Licensing Board or Board of Accounting annual renewal fees. Other examples include insurance agent's renewal licensing fees or real estate agent licensee renewal fees.

53. OCCUPATIONAL TAXES

You can deduct an occupational tax charged at a flat rate by a locality for the privilege of working or conducting a business in the locality. If you are an employee, you can claim occupational taxes only as a miscellaneous deduction subject to the 2% limit; you cannot claim them as a deduction for taxes elsewhere on your return.

54. RESEARCH EXPENSES OF A COLLEGE PROFESSOR

If you are a college professor, you can deduct your research expenses, including travel expenses, for teaching, lecturing, or writing and publishing on subjects that relate directly to your teaching duties.

You must have undertaken the research as a means of carrying out the duties expected of a professor and without expectation of profit, apart from salary. However, you cannot deduct the cost of travel as a form of education. Of course, the expenses must be paid by you, not by the University where you are employed.

55. TOOLS USED IN YOUR WORK

If your job requires special tools that your employer does not provide to you then you may be able to deduct the cost. How the cost is deducted depends on the useful life of the tools.

Generally, you can deduct amounts you spend for tools used in your work if the tools wear out and are thrown away within 1 year from the date of purchase. You can depreciate the cost of tools that have a useful life substantially beyond the one year. As always, you have to pay for the tools, not your employer.

For example, a hairdresser may need special clippers or scissors, or a carpenter who has to purchase his own hammer. If they are predicted to last less than a year you would deduct all of the cost in the year of purchase. If they are predicted to last much longer than a year then they would be depreciated over the useful life of the item.

Alternatively, you may be able to use a Section 179 depreciation deduction, which would allow you to deduct the entire cost in the year of purchase even if the useful life was greater than one year.

56. TRAVEL

You can deduct travel expenses that you pay while traveling away from home for your employer. You have to pay for the travel, and can't be reimbursed by your employer. You can deduct travel expenses paid or incurred in connection with a temporary work assignment. Generally, you can't deduct travel expenses paid in connection with an indefinite work assignment.

It is considered to be a temporary assignment is if it is realistically expected to last for a year or less in a single location.

The travel expenses that you can deduct include: the cost of getting to and from the business destination, this can by via plane, train, bus, and car. You can also deduct the costs of meals and lodging while you are away from home. Taxi fares, baggage charges, and cleaning and laundry expenses are also allowable.

In 2011 1.7 million taxpayers had unreimbursed employee travel expenses, averaging almost $2,900 each.

57. LOCAL TRANSPORTATION EXPENSES

You can deduct your local transportation expenses related to getting from one workplace to another when you are not traveling away from home. According to IRS regulations these expenses can be include the cost of transportation by train, bus, tax, car, or plain. Although I'm not sure how you would travel by plane and not be away from home. If you are using your own car, the standard mileage rate is 56 cents per mile.

An example of this is if you are a carpenter working for a construction company, and you drive your own car from one construction site to another. It would not include driving to and from your home. But, if you work at two or more place in one day, whether or not it's for the same employer, generally you can deduct the expenses of getting from one workplace to the other.

Local transportation expenses are more common than out-out-town travel, as 4.8 million taxpayers claimed this expenses deduction in 2011. The average for those taxpayers was over $6,500 each.

58. TRAVEL FROM YOUR HOME OFFICE

There is one exception to the rule that you can't deduct the cost of driving from your home to a workplace. That is, if your principle place of business is in your home, then you can deduct the cost of going from your home to other work places associated with your employment.

You may also deduct the cost of going between your residence and a temporary work location outside of the area where you live and normally work. If you have one or more regular work locations away from your residence, you may also deduct the cost of going between your residence and a temporary work location in the same trade or business within your metropolitan area.

59. MEALS AND ENTERTAINMENT

Generally, you can deduct entertainment expenses (including entertainment-related meals) only if they are directly related to the active conduct of your trade or business. However, the expense only needs to be associated with the active conduct of your trade or business if it directly precedes or follows a substantial and bona fide business-related discussion.

So if you meet a client at your office, and have a meeting about his business with the company you work for, then you take the client out for lunch. The cost of the meals would be deductible for you, assuming the cost isn't reimbursed by your employer.

For employees who have unreimbursed meal or entertainment expenses this can be a significant deduction. In 2011, 2.9 million taxpayers claimed this deduction, with an average expense of over $3,500.

60. GIFT EXPENSES

If you give gifts in the course of your business, you will be able to deduct either all or part of the costs. You can generally deduct up to $25 of business gifts that you give to any one person during the year. Before you scoff at the amount, consider this, if you give your top one hundred clients a $25 gift each. You would be able to deduct $2,500.

Let's look at an example.

If you give one of your business customers three gift baskets to thank them for their business, and you paid $$90 for each basket, or $270 total. Three of the business's executives took the gift baskets home for their families' use. You would be able to deduct a total of $75, 3 x $25, for the gift baskets.

If there are incident costs, like engraving on jewelry, or mailing costs, these costs are generally not included for the purpose of the $25 limit.

Identical, widely distributed promotional items, costing $4 or less do not count toward the $25 limit as long as your name is clearly and permanently printed on the items.

61. HOME-OFFICE DEDUCTION – FOR EMPLOYEES

If you are an employee and you use a part of your home for business, you may qualify for a deduction for its business use. You must meet the general home-office requirements, plus:

- Your business use must be for the convenience of your employer, and

- You must not rent any part of your home to your employer and use the rented portion to perform services as an employee for that employer.

If the use of the home office is merely appropriate and helpful, you cannot deduct expenses for the business use of your home.

Another way for employees to claim the home office deduction is if you rent the area you use for work in your home to your employer. Personally, I haven't run across this being done, but it is an option.

62. LOCAL LODGING

Normally, any lodging expenses you have while not traveling away from home are considered personal expenses and are not deductible.

However, under new IRS regulations if your employer requires you to obtain lodging while you are not traveling away from home, you can deduct the costs if it is just temporary, if it is necessary for you to participate in or be available for a business meeting or employer function and the costs are ordinary and necessary. For example, your employer is hosting an event at a local resort for the firm's top clients and you need to be available to assist clients, you could deduct the cost of lodging if you paid and not your employer.

Other examples given in the IRS regulations to illustrate the facts-and-circumstances test include employees who are required to stay at a local hotel during a work-related training session; professional athletes who are required to stay at a local hotel before a home game; an employee who is relocating for work and looking for a new home; an employee who has to stay at a hotel near the office while working long hours; and employees who occasionally are on call for a night duty shift and stay at a local hotel.

63. UNION DUES

You can deduct any union dues or initiation fees you pay for union membership. You may also deduct any assessments you pay for benefit payments to unemployed union members.

However, you cannot deduct the part of the assessments or contributions that provides funds for the payment of sick, accident, or death benefits. Also, you cannot deduct contributions to a pension fund even if the union requires you to make the contributions.

You also may not be able to deduct amounts you pay to the union that are related to certain lobbying and political activities.

64. WORK CLOTHES AND UNIFORMS

You can deduct the costs of your work clothes as long as you meet the following two requirements. You have to wear them as a condition of your employment, and the clothes are not suitable for everyday wear. It is not enough that you wear distinctive clothing. It must specifically be required by your employer. It's also not enough that, you don't wear your work clothes away from work. The work clothing can't be suitable for taking the place of your regular clothes.

A real life example that has been making news lately, is Walmart instituting a new dress code. The new dress code is requiring workers to wear blue collared shirts and khaki pants. Even though required by the company, this would not meet the requirement to be deductible because they are suitable for everyday wear.

Examples of workers who may be able to deduct the cost and upkeep of work clothes are: delivery workers, firefighters, health care workers, police officers, letter carriers, professional athletes, and transportation workers. However, work clothing consisting of white cap, white shirt or white jacket, white bib overalls, and standard work shoes, which a painter is required by his union to wear on the job, is not distinctive in character or in the nature of a uniform. Similarly, the costs of buying and maintaining blue work clothes worn by a welder at the request of a foreman are not deductible.

65. PROTECTIVE CLOTHING

If you work in a profession that is inherently dangerous, such as construction, steam fitting and oil field work, purchasing protective clothing to wear on the job is essential, and in many cases required.

Deductible protective clothing can include hard hats, construction boots, safety glasses, work gloves, fire-retardant outerwear and any other article of clothing that protects against the common health hazards of your profession

Other examples of workers who may be required to wear safety items include: carpenters, cement workers, chemical workers, electricians, fishing boat crew members, machinists, pipe fitters, steamfitters, and truck drivers.

Police officers or other law enforcement personnel are able to deduct the costs of bullet-proof vest if they had to purchase the vest instead of it being provided by their department.

66. GAMBLING LOSSES

As you may know, any gambling winnings you have are fully taxable and have to be reported on your tax return. Gambling isn't just playing cards or betting on a game. It includes winnings from lotteries, raffles, horse races, and casinos as well. In addition, it's not just cash winnings, it also includes the value of prizes like cars and trips.

The good news is that any gambling losses you have can be deducted if you itemize deductions. The amount of losses you can deduct is limited to the amount of gambling income you report on your return. This deduction doesn't impact many taxpayers, only about 900,000 claimed the deduction in 2011. However, for those who do claim the deduction, the deduction averages over $19,500.

It is important to keep an accurate diary or similar record of your gambling winnings and losses. To deduct your losses, you must be able to provide receipts, tickets, statements or other records that show the amount of both your winnings and losses.

67. SELECTED BUSINESS DEDUCTIONS

Most of this book thus far has been devoted to deductions and credits available to taxpayers in general, now I want to provide some guidance to those taxpayers who own a small business and report their business income and expenses on Schedule C of their tax returns. I won't cover every business expense, but I do want to cover a few of the more complex areas and areas that the IRS focuses their audit efforts on.

I am going to cover the home-office deduction, car and truck expenses, and travel, meals, and entertainment in detail because these deductions have very complex rules and requirements for claiming the expenses deduction, and because the IRS focuses on these expenses during an audit.

For those taxpayers who are required to file a Schedule C, you can take comfort in the fact that you are not alone in this requirement. In 2011, which is the most recent data available, about 26.1 million tax returns included a Schedule C. About 18 percent of all returns filed, that means almost one in five American taxpayers own a small business that requires filing a Schedule C.

While you are not alone, filing a Schedule C, or Schedule C-EZ does greatly increase your chance of an IRS audit. Overall the IRS audits about one percent of all individual tax returns in recent years. However, for those who filed a Schedule C with gross receipts of over $100,000 the audit rate increase over 470% to about 4.7 percent. Keep in mind the $100,000 is from total gross income, before any business expenses are deducted. For 2010, a total of 277,945 sole proprietors had their tax returns audited. This was over 16% of all IRS audits for the year.

You probably didn't know that the IRS has developed special audit technique guides for various industries. These guides were developed to assist the IRS auditors in performing audit examinations. These guides contain examination techniques, industry issues, business practices, industry terminology, and other information to assist examiners in performing audits for particular industries. The most important thing is to make sure that any business expense that you list on your Schedule C, is an actual legitimate expense.

Below are some of the key items that can trigger an IRS audit of your tax return.

The business use of your car is an area that the IRS pays close attention to. It is an area where they actually spell out the type of records you need to keep to track the use of your car. Many people get into trouble trying to claim that they use their car 100% for business purposes when in fact they also use it for non-business purposes. IRS agents are trained to focus on this issue and know how to probe to disallow your deduction.

Another business deduction that can trigger a closer look from the IRS is the home-office deduction. There are certain rules that must be followed to claim this deduction. Make sure you know the requirements and keep good records. I'll go into detail a little later about the exact requirements. This can be a good deduction, but there is a risk involved.

Finally, claiming business meals, travel and entertainment can be a red flag to the IRS. Again, the IRS has strict rules and substantiation requirements. Be sure any of these expenses that you claim are actual business expenses and that you understand what the rules are and keep good records.

Let's talk a little about which of your expenses can be deducted as a business expense. Business expenses are the costs associated with operating a trade or business, and they are usually deductible if the business is operated to make a profit. According to IRS regulations, a business expense must be ordinary and necessary expenses for the carrying on of a trade or business, or for the production of income.

Unfortunately, the words "ordinary and necessary" are not defined in the IRS Code or regulations. However, some of the elements have been defined, these are listed below:

- The expenses must be incurred in an existing business. Start-up or investigatory expenses for a new business are not deductible, but must be amortized over 180 months.

- The expense must be normal, usual, or customary to the business involved and appropriate and helpful to the business activity when incurred.

- The expense must actually be paid or incurred under the business's accounting method

- Lavish or extravagant entertainment expenses are not deductible. However, entertainment expenses are not disallowed just because they exceed a certain dollar amount or are from expensive restaurants, hotels, nightclubs, or resorts. An expense is not lavish or extravagant if when considering the all facts and circumstances it is reasonable

The following list of items are not currently deductible, they are either not deductible at all or receive special tax treatment.

- Personal Expenses
- Passive losses
- At-risk amounts
- Capital Expenses
- Expenses used to compute cost of goods sold

68. BUSINESS VS. PERSONAL EXPENSES

The general rule is that, a business owner cannot deduct personal living expenses. However, if there is an expense for something that is used partly for business and partly for personal purposes, the total cost can be divided between the business and personal parts, and the business portion may be deducted.

So, you can't deduct the cost of your groceries, or your clothing, or any other expense that does not directly benefit your business.

However, if a business owner borrows money and uses 60 percent of it for the business and the remaining 40 percent for personal expenses, then 60 percent of the interest is deductible as a business expense. The remaining 40 percent is personal interest and is not deductible.

69. PASSIVE LOSSES

Generally, you are in a passive activity if you have a trade or business activity in which you do not materially participate, or a rental activity. In general, deductions for losses from passive activities offset income only from passive activities. Any excess deductions cannot be used to offset other income. In addition, passive activity credits can offset the tax only on net passive income. Any excess loss or credits are carried over to later years.

It is easy to determine whether you have income or loss from real estate rentals. But the concept of "material participation" is more complicated. According to the IRS, you materially participate in a business only if you are involved with its day-to-day operations on a regular, continuous, and substantial basis. The IRS has created several tests to determine material participation, based on the amount of time you spend working at it.

For example, a person who owns and spends all of his or her time running a business actively participates in the business. The income or loss that person incurs from the business is active, not passive. On the other hand, a person who invests in a business, but spends no time at all actually working in the business, does not materially participate in the business. His or her income or loss from the business is passive income or loss.

This is an important difference. Because you can deduct passive losses only from passive income, not from income from other sources such as earnings from a job or a business you actively manage.

For example, you are a successful lawyer. This year, you have $250,000 in income from your practice and you also earn $40,000 in income from investments. You invest $35,000 in a real estate limited partnership tax shelter. The partnership owns several rental properties that operate at a substantial loss. At the end of the year, the partnership informs you that your share of the partnership's annual operating loss is $55,000. Sidney invested in the limited partnership because he wanted to use his share of the losses it generated to reduce his taxable income from his medical practice. However, come tax time, you are in for a shock. Because passive losses are only deductible from passive income, you cannot deduct his $55,000 passive loss from his law practice income or his investment income. You earned no passive income during the year so you can't use your passive loss at all this year. Your real estate tax shelter turned out to be useless.

70. CAPITAL EXPENSES

Businesses must capitalize some costs, rather than deduct them as expenses. That means that these costs become part of the investment in the business and are called "capital expenses." Capital expenses are considered assets of a business. In general, there are three types of costs that must be capitalized:

(1) Business start-up costs,

(2) Business assets, and

(3) Improvements.

A business can elect to deduct as an expense, up to $5,000 of start-up costs that are paid or incurred. The remaining costs can be amortized over 180 months.

The IRS views capital expenses as investments in the business, rather than as an expenses of the business. The money hasn't really left the business, it was just transformed into another type of asset.

A good rule-of-thumb is that, if a business expects to use something for more than a year it should be capitalized.

71. BUSINESS EXPENSES THAT ARE DEDUCTIBLE

I have talked briefly about the types of expenses that are not allowed to be deducted as business expenses, now let's take a look at the expenses that you can deduct. The Schedule C lists 23 categories of expenses, not including the deduction for the business use of your home, which is listed separately. Most small business owners won't have expenses in every category, but I'll list them all here so that you can see all the types of expenses that are deductible as business expenses.

The categories of expenses are:

- Advertising

- Car and truck expenses

- Commissions and fees

- Contract labor

- Depletion

- Depreciation and section 179 expense
- Employee benefit programs
- Insurance(other than health)
- Interest
    - Mortgage
    - Other
- Legal and professional services
- Office Expense
- Pension and profit-sharing plans
- Rent or lease
    - Vehicles, machinery, and equipment
    - Other business property
- Repairs and maintenance
- Supplies
- Taxes and licenses
- Travel, meals, and entertainment
    - Travel
    - Deductible meals and entertainment
- Utilities

- Wages

- Other expenses

72. ADVERTISING

As a small business owner, I'm sure you are aware that if you have advertising expenses, that you are allowed to deduct them. What you may not know if all of the different kinds of expenses that go into this category. Of course advertising expenses include things like radio and television ads, and newspaper advertising. It also includes the costs of developing and hosting your website, as well as any pay-per-click advertising that you do online.

In addition, if you do any direct mailing, the costs of postage, envelops, stationary, and postage is included, as is the cost of business cards and numerous other items.

In 2011, of the 26.1 million Schedule Cs filed, 5.7 million included advertising expenses, with the average expense totaling about $2,350.

73. OFFICE EXPENSE

For tax purposes what's the difference between office expenses and office supplies? You should think of office expenses as the costs that are not part of your everyday use of tangible supplies.

This would include utilities such as electricity, heating, and phone. Office expenses can also include improvement purchases such as new carpeting, lighting and paint. In addition, if you purchase new equipment like a printer or computer, or new furniture like a desk and chair, you can include those purchases in your office expenses.

This would also include charges like a desk fee for real estate agents.

74. SUPPLIES

As mentioned in the previous section, office expenses as the costs that are not part of your everyday use of tangible supplies.

That leaves us to talk about those supplies that are used up in the day to day running of your business. Supplies include are any business items that are used up in one year or less. This would include things like paper, pens, paperclips, staples and postage stamps not used for marketing. Small, inexpensive items you may not replace frequently are also considered office supplies, like staplers and mouse pads.

Do not include promotional items in your office supplies expenses. If you give out promotional pens, they would be considered an advertising expense.

IRS records indicate that 9.2 million Schedule Cs included supplies expenses in 2011, averaging almost $3,500 per Schedule C.

75. TAXES AND LICENSES

There are several types of taxes and licenses that can be included in this expense category.

If you have employees, you can deduct the cost of Social Security tax and Medicare tax paid on employee wages. You can also deduct as business expanses, personal property taxes on any business assets.

Any licenses or regulatory fees paid to state or local governments also go here as well. For example this is where I would report the CPA renewal fee that I pay to the West Virginia and Virginia Boards of Accountancy.

I also have to pay a Business & Occupation (B&O) tax to the City of Morgantown. That is included in this category as well.

Do not deduct federal income tax or your self-employment tax here. However, you do get to deduct half of your self-employment tax on your 1040, on line 27.

76. SELF-EMPLOYED HEALTH INSURANCE DEDUCTION

As a self-employed individual, you may be able to deduct the cost of your health insurance for yourself and family, including your children under the age of 27. Premiums for medical insurance, dental insurance and long-term care insurance are deductible.

You cannot claim the deduction for any month in which you are eligible to participate in health coverage provided by your or your spouse's employer. Or the employer of your child.

Your deduction is limited to your self-employment income, minus the 50% deduction for self-employment taxes, minus any retirement plan contributions. The remainder is the maximum allowable amount of deductions for health insurance expenses.

If you have a net loss for a year from your business, you can't deduct any of the costs of your health insurance coverage.

Although over 26 million taxpayers filed a Schedule C in 2011, only 3.8 million claimed the self-employed health insurance deduction. I think three factors account for this; many people who own a small business requiring the Schedule C filing also have a another job which may provide insurance coverage; the second is that their spouse may provide the health insurance coverage through their employer; lastly some probably just can't afford it.

This expense is not reported on Schedule C like most of your other business expenses, it is an "above the line" deduction on Form 1040 on Line 29.

77. HOME-OFFICE DEDUCTION IF SELF-EMPLOYED

The home-office deduction is probably the one deduction that causes the most angst for both the small-business owner and their accountants. On one hand the home-office deduction can be a big money saver, on the other hand it can also flag you for an IRS audit. It becomes a question of risk versus reward.

If you play by the rules and keep good records, you can stand up to the IRS and save large amounts on your taxes with this deduction. The deduction is especially valuable, if you use the home office year after year. In 2011, about 3.3 million taxpayers claimed the deduction for the business use of their home. For these taxpayers the average deduction amount was just over $3,000. You can see why the IRS looks closely at this deduction when you see the dollar amounts, combined with the fact that many taxpayers abuse this deduction.

Let's look at the requirements for claiming the home-office deduction. In order for a portion of the expenses of a residence to be allocated to your business, you must prove that a portion of the home is used "exclusively and regularly for business purposes". The space must meet one of the following requirements, you must show that you use your home as your principal place of business. If you conduct business at a location outside of your home, but also use your home substantially and regularly to conduct business, you may qualify for a home office deduction. For example, if you have in-person meetings with patients, clients, or customers in your home in the normal course of your business, even though you also carry on business at another location, you can deduct your expenses for the part of your home used exclusively and regularly for business. You can deduct expenses for a separate free-standing structure, such as a studio, garage, or barn, if you use it exclusively and regularly for your business. The structure does not have to be your principal place of business or the only place where you meet patients, clients, or customers.

Generally, deductions for a home office are based on the percentage of your home devoted to business use. So, if you use a whole room or part of a room for conducting your business, you need to figure out the percentage of your home devoted to your business activities. This is done by taking the square footage of the space used for business and divide by the total square footage in the home.

Exclusive Use Requirement

Let's look at the exclusive use requirement. You don't have to have an entire room set aside for the business, it just means that you can't use the area for other activities. This is actually a hard requirement to meet. Let me give some examples of activates that will disallow the deduction due to this requirement not being met.

Let's say you have a small room in your house where you have set up a small office. It has a desk, a phone, a computer and filing cabinet. You use the office on a daily basis. It is your only place of business. Occasionally, your child uses the computer to do homework. You will have failed the exclusivity requirement.

Another example, let's assume the same facts as above. Except this time, your child never uses the computer. However, you do use the room to store Christmas decorations. Congratulations, you have again failed the "exclusive use" requirement.

As you can see the exclusive use requirement is actually very difficult to meet even if you are aware of the requirements.

Exceptions to Exclusive Use Requirement

There are a couple of exceptions to the exclusive use requirements. If you run a daycare facility from your home. The care can be for children, physically or mentally handicapped, or individuals 65 or older. The other exception is if you use part of your home to store inventory that is held for sale. This exception only applies if the home is your only location of the business.

For example, your home is the only fixed location of your business of selling mechanics' tools at retail. You regularly use half of your basement for storage of inventory and product samples. You sometimes use the area for personal purposes. The expenses for the storage space are deductible even though you do not use this part of your basement exclusively for business.

Regular Use Requirement

To qualify under the regular use test, you must use a specific area of your home for business on a regular basis. Incidental or occasional business use is not regular use. You must consider all facts and circumstances in determining whether your use is on a regular basis.

Trade or Business Use Requirement

To qualify under the trade-or-business-use test, you must use part of your home in connection with a trade or business. If you use your home for a profit-seeking activity that is not a trade or business, you cannot take a deduction for its business use.

For example, you use part of your home exclusively and regularly to read financial periodicals and reports, clip bond coupons, and carry out similar activities related to your own investments. You do not make investments as a broker or dealer. So, your activities are not part of a trade or business and you cannot take a deduction for the business use of your home.

Principle Place of Business

This is an important issue for many real estate agents, due to the fact that many agents have desk space at their brokers' place of business. It can also be a common issue for doctors who are provided office space by the hospital where they work, but also have a home office. IRS regulations state that you can have more than one business location, including your home, for a single business. To qualify to deduct the expenses for the business use of your home under the principal place of business test, your home must be your principal place of business for that business. To determine whether your home is your principal place of business, you must consider the following factors:

- The relative importance of the activities performed at each place where you conduct business, and

- The amount of time spent at each place where you conduct business.

Your home office will qualify as your principal place of business if you meet the following requirements.

- You use it exclusively and regularly for administrative or management activities of your trade or business.

- You have no other fixed location where you conduct substantial administrative or management activities of your trade or business.

If, after considering your business locations, your home cannot be identified as your principal place of business, you cannot deduct home office expenses.

You may be wondering what qualifies as administrative or management activities for this purpose. There are many activities that are administrative or managerial in nature. The following are a few examples.

- Billing customers, clients, or patients.

- Keeping books and records.

- Ordering supplies.

- Setting up appointments.

- Forwarding orders or writing reports.

What if you also perform administrative or management activities at other locations? The following activities performed by you or others will not disqualify your home office from being your principal place of business.

- You have others conduct your administrative or management activities at locations other than your home. (For example, another company does your billing from its place of business.)

- You conduct administrative or management activities at places that are not fixed locations of your business, such as in a car, restaurant, or hotel room.

- You occasionally conduct minimal administrative or management activities at a fixed location outside your home.

- You conduct substantial non-administrative or non-management business activities at a fixed location outside your home. (For example, you meet with or provide services to customers, clients, or patients at a fixed location of the business outside your home.)

- You have suitable space to conduct administrative or management activities outside your home, but choose to use your home office for those activities instead.

Here are some examples to help demonstrate when home office expenses can be deducted

Example

Jenny is a self-employed real estate agent. Desk space is provided by her broker. Jenny also has a small home-office. Jenny meets clients at the broker's office and sometimes shows them properties on the office computer there. Jenny performs all the administrative work from her home-office. She would be allowed to deduct the home-office expense.

However, if she did the administrative work at both locations equally, or even regularly at the brokers office, even if she did more at home, she wouldn't be able to take the home-office deduction.

Your particular situation in its entirety needs to be taken into account to determine whether you can deduct your home-office expense.

Example

John is a self-employed plumber. Most of John's time is spent at customers' homes and offices installing and repairing plumbing. He has a small office in his home that he uses exclusively and regularly for the administrative or management activities of his business, such as phoning customers, ordering supplies, and keeping his books.

John writes up estimates and records of work completed at his customers' premises. He does not conduct any substantial administrative or management activities at any fixed location other than his home office. John does not do his own billing. He uses a local bookkeeping service to bill his customers.

John's home office qualifies as his principal place of business for deducting expenses for its use. He uses the home office for the administrative or managerial activities of his plumbing business and he has no other fixed location where he conducts these administrative or managerial activities. His choice to have his billing done by another company does not disqualify his home office from being his principal place of business. He meets all the qualifications, including principal place of business, so he can deduct expenses (subject to certain limitations, explained later) for the business use of his home.

Example

Pamela is a self-employed sales representative for several different product lines. She has an office in her home that she uses exclusively and regularly to set up appointments and write up orders and other reports for the companies whose products she sells. She occasionally writes up orders and sets up appointments from her hotel room when she is away on business overnight.

Pamela's business is selling products to customers at various locations throughout her territory. To make these sales, she regularly visits customers to explain the available products and take orders.

Pamela's home office qualifies as her principal place of business for deducting expenses for its use. She conducts administrative or management activities there and she has no other fixed location where she conducts substantial administrative or management activities. The fact that she conducts some administrative or management activities in her hotel room (not a fixed location) does not disqualify her home office from being her principal place of business. She meets all the qualifications, including principal place of business, so she can deduct expenses (subject to certain limitations, explained later) for the business use of her home.

Example

Paul is a self-employed anesthesiologist. He spends the majority of his time administering anesthesia and postoperative care in three local hospitals. One of the hospitals provides him with a small shared office where he could conduct administrative or management activities.

Paul very rarely uses the office the hospital provides. He uses a room in his home that he has converted to an office. He uses this room exclusively and regularly to conduct all the following activities.

- Contacting patients, surgeons, and hospitals regarding scheduling.
- Preparing for treatments and presentations.
- Maintaining billing records and patient logs.
- Satisfying continuing medical education requirements.
- Reading medical journals and books.

Paul's home office qualifies as his principal place of business for deducting expenses for its use. He conducts administrative or management activities for his business as an anesthesiologist there and he has no other fixed location where he conducts substantial administrative or management activities for this business. His choice to use his home office instead of the one provided by the hospital does not disqualify his home office from being his principal place of business. His performance of substantial non-administrative or non-management activities at fixed locations outside his home also does not disqualify his home office from being his principal place of business. He meets all the qualifications, including principal place of business, so he can deduct expenses (subject to certain limitations, explained later) for the business use of his home.

Example

Kathleen is employed as a teacher. She is required to teach and meet with students at the school and to grade papers and tests. The school provides her with a small office where she can work on her lesson plans, grade papers and tests, and meet with parents and students. The school does not require her to work at home.

Kathleen prefers to use the office she has set up in her home and does not use the one provided by the school. She uses this home office exclusively and regularly for the administrative duties of her teaching job.

Kathleen must meet the convenience-of-the-employer test, even if her home qualifies as her principal place of business for deducting expenses for its use. Her employer provides her with an office and does not require her to work at home, so she does not meet the convenience-of-the-employer test and cannot claim a deduction for the business use of her home.

More Than One Business

The same home office can be the principal place of business for two or more separate business activities. Whether your home office is the principal place of business for more than one business activity must be determined separately for each of your trade or business activities. You must use the home office exclusively and regularly for one or more of the following purposes.

- As the principal place of business for one or more of your trades or businesses.
- As a place to meet or deal with patients, clients, or customers in the normal course of one or more of your trades or businesses.
- If your home office is a separate structure, in connection with one or more of your trades or businesses.

You can use your home office for more than one business activity, but you cannot use it for any non-business (i.e., personal) activities.

Place To Meet Patients, Clients, or Customers

If you meet or deal with patients, clients, or customers in your home in the normal course of your business, even though you also carry on business at another location, you can deduct your expenses for the part of your home used exclusively and regularly for business if you meet both the following tests.

- You physically meet with patients, clients, or customers on your premises.
- Their use of your home is substantial and integral to the conduct of your business.

Doctors, dentists, attorneys, and other professionals who maintain offices in their homes generally will meet this requirement.

Using your home for occasional meetings and telephone calls will not qualify you to deduct expenses for the business use of your home.

The part of your home you use exclusively and regularly to meet patients, clients, or customers does not have to be your principal place of business.

Example.

Jane Atwood, a self-employed attorney, works 3 days a week in her city office. She works 2 days a week in her home office used only for business. She regularly meets clients there. Her home office qualifies for a business deduction because she meets clients there in the normal course of her business.

Separate Structure

You can deduct expenses for a separate free-standing structure, such as a studio, workshop, garage, or barn, if you use it exclusively and regularly for your business. The structure does not have to be your principal place of business or a place where you meet patients, clients, or customers.

Example.

John Smith operates a floral shop in town. He grows the plants for his shop in a greenhouse behind his home. He uses the greenhouse exclusively and regularly in his business, so he can deduct the expenses for its use, subject to certain limitations, explained later.

Computing the Deduction Amount

Once you have determined that you qualify for the home-office deduction you can begin to compute the amount you can deduct for the business use of your home.

Beginning with tax year 2013, for returns filed in 2014, taxpayers have the option of using the simplified option, or the actual expense method when figuring the deduction for the business use of their home. The simplified option doesn't change the criteria for who may claim a home office deduction. It just simplifies the calculation and recordkeeping requirements of the allowable deduction.

Highlights of the simplified option:

- Standard deduction of $5 per square foot of home used for business (maximum 300 square feet).
- Allowable home-related itemized deductions claimed in full on Schedule A. (For example: Mortgage interest, real estate taxes).
- No home depreciation deduction or later recapture of depreciation for the years the simplified option is used.

Comparison of methods

Simplified Option	Regular Method
Deduction for home office use of a portion of a residence allowed only if that portion is **exclusively** used on a **regular basis** for business purposes	Same
Allowable square footage of home use for business (not to exceed 300 square feet)	Percentage of home used for business
Standard $5 per square foot used to determine home business deduction	Actual expenses determined and records maintained
Home-related itemized deductions claimed in full on Schedule A	Home-related itemized deductions apportioned between Schedule A and business schedule (Sch. C or Sch. F)
No depreciation deduction	Depreciation deduction for portion of home used for business
No recapture of depreciation upon sale of home	Recapture of depreciation on gain upon sale of home
Deduction cannot exceed gross income from business use of home, less business expenses	Same
Amount in excess of gross income limitation may **not** be carried over	Amount in excess of gross income limitation may be carried over
Loss carryover from use of regular method in prior year may **not** be claimed	Loss carryover from use of regular method in prior year may be claimed if gross income test is met in current year

Selecting a Method

- You may choose to use either the simplified method or the regular method for any taxable year.
- You choose a method by simply by using that method on federal income tax return for the taxable year.
- Once you have chosen a method for a taxable year, you cannot later change to the other method for that same year.
- If you use the simplified method for one year and use the regular method for any subsequent year, you must calculate the depreciation deduction for the subsequent year using the appropriate optional depreciation table. This is true regardless of whether you used an optional depreciation table for the first year the property was used in business.

Using Actual Expenses

If you do not or cannot elect to use the simplified method for a home, you will figure your deduction for that home using your actual expenses. You will also need to figure the percentage of your home used for business and the limit on the deduction.

You cannot deduct expenses for the business use of your home incurred during any part of the year you did not use your home for business purposes. For example, if you begin using part of your home for business on July 1, and you meet all the tests from that date until the end of the year, you only get to include your expenses for the last half of the year in figuring your allowable deduction.

You have to divide the expenses of operating your home between personal and business use. The part of a home operating expense you can use to figure your deduction depends on both of the following.

- Whether the expense is direct, indirect, or unrelated.
- The percentage of your home used for business.

The Table below describes the types of expenses you may have and the extent to which they are deductible.

Types of Expenses

Expense	Description	Deductibility
Direct	Expenses only for the business part of your home.	Deductible in full.
	Examples: Painting or repairs only in the area used for business.	Exception: May be only partially deductible in a daycare facility.
Indirect	Expenses for keeping up and running your entire home.	Deductible based on the percentage of your home used for business.
	Examples: Insurance, utilities, and general repairs.	
Unrelated	Expenses only for the parts of your home not used for business.	Not deductible.
	Examples: Lawn care or painting a room not used for business.	

Certain expenses are deductible whether or not you use your home for business. If you qualify to deduct business use of the home expenses, use the business percentage of these expenses to figure your total business use of the home deduction. These expenses include the following.

- Real estate taxes.
- Qualified mortgage insurance premiums.
- Deductible mortgage interest.
- Casualty losses.

Other expenses are deductible only if you use your home for business. You can use the business percentage of these expenses to figure your total business use of the home deduction. These expenses generally include (but are not limited to) the following.

- Depreciation.
- Insurance.
- Rent paid for the use of property you do not own but use in your trade or business.
- Repairs.
- Security system.
- Utilities and services.

Let's look at each of these expenses:

Real estate taxes

To figure the business part of your real estate taxes, multiply the real estate taxes paid by the percentage of your home used for business.

Qualified mortgage insurance premiums

To figure the business part of your qualified mortgage insurance premiums, multiply the premiums by the percentage of your home used for business. You can include premiums for insurance on a second mortgage in this computation. If your adjusted gross income is more than $100,000 ($50,000 if your filing status is married filing separately), your deduction may be limited.

Deductible mortgage interest

To figure the business part of your deductible mortgage interest, multiply this interest by the percentage of your home used for business. You can include interest on a second mortgage in this computation. If your total mortgage debt is more than $1,000,000 or your home equity debt is more than $100,000, your deduction may be limited.

Casualty losses

If you have a casualty loss on your home that you use for business, you can treat the casualty loss as a direct expense, an indirect expense, or an unrelated expense, depending on the property affected.

- A direct expense is the loss on the portion of the property you use only in your business. Use the entire loss to figure the business use of the home deduction.
- An indirect expense is the loss on property you use for both business and personal purposes. Use only the business portion to figure the deduction.
- An unrelated expense is the loss on property you do not use in your business. Do not use any of the loss to figure the deduction.

Insurance

You can deduct the cost of insurance that covers the business part of your home. However, if your insurance premium gives you coverage for a period that extends past the end of your tax year, you can deduct only the business percentage of the part of the premium that gives you coverage for your tax year. You can deduct the business percentage of the part that applies to the following year in that year.

Rent

If you rent your home and meet the requirements for business use of the home, you can deduct part of the rent you pay. To figure your deduction, multiply your rent payments by the percentage of your home used for business.

Repairs

The cost of repairs that relate to your business, including labor, not counting your own labor, is a deductible expense. For example, a furnace repair benefits the entire home. If you use 10% of your home for business, you can deduct 10% of the cost of the furnace repair.

Repairs keep your home in good working order over its useful life. Examples of common repairs are patching walls and floors, painting, wallpapering, repairing roofs and gutters, and mending leaks. However, repairs are sometimes treated as a permanent improvement and are not deductible.

Security system

If you install a security system that protects all the doors and windows in your home, you can deduct the business part of the expenses you incur to maintain and monitor the system. You also can take a depreciation deduction for the part of the cost of the security system relating to the business use of your home.

Utilities and services

Expenses for utilities and services, such as electricity, gas, trash removal, and cleaning services, are primarily personal expenses. However, if you use part of your home for business, you can deduct the business part of these expenses. Generally, the business percentage for utilities is the same as the percentage of your home used for business.

Telephone

The basic local telephone service charge, including taxes, for the first telephone line into your home (i.e., landline) is a nondeductible personal expense. However, charges for business long-distance phone calls on that line, as well as the cost of a second line into your home used exclusively for business, are deductible business expenses. Do not include these expenses as a cost of using your home for business. Deduct these charges separately. For example, if you file

Schedule C, deduct these expenses on line 25, Utilities (instead of line 30, Expenses for business use of your home).

Depreciating Your Home

If you own your home and qualify to deduct expenses for its business use, you can claim a deduction for depreciation. Depreciation is an allowance for the wear and tear on the part of your home used for business. You cannot depreciate the cost or value of the land. You recover the cost of the land when you sell or otherwise dispose of the property.

Before you figure your depreciation deduction, you need to know the following information.

- The month and year you started using your home for business.
- The adjusted basis and fair market value of your home (excluding land) at the time you began using it for business.
- The cost of any improvements before and after you began using the property for business.
- The percentage of your home used for business.

Adjusted basis defined.

The adjusted basis of your home is generally its cost, plus the cost of any permanent improvements you made to it, minus any casualty losses or depreciation deducted in earlier tax years.

Permanent improvements.

A permanent improvement increases the value of property, adds to its life, or gives it a new or different use. Examples of improvements are replacing electric wiring or plumbing, adding a new roof or addition, paneling, or remodeling.

You have to be careful to distinguish between repairs and improvements. You also must keep accurate records of these expenses. These records will help you decide whether an expense is a deductible or a capital (added to the basis) expense. However, if you make repairs as part of an extensive remodeling or restoration of your home, the entire job is an improvement.

Example.

You buy an older home and fix up two rooms as a beauty salon. You patch the plaster on the ceilings and walls, paint, repair the floor, install an outside door, and install new wiring, plumbing, and other equipment. Normally, the patching, painting, and floor work are repairs and the other expenses are permanent improvements. However, because the work gives your property a new use, the entire remodeling job is a permanent improvement and its cost is added to the basis of the property. You cannot deduct any portion of it as a repair expense.

Adjusting for depreciation deducted in earlier years.

Decrease the basis of your property by the depreciation you deducted, or could have deducted, on your tax returns under the method of depreciation you properly selected. If you deducted less depreciation than you could have under the method you selected, decrease the basis by the amount you could have deducted under that method. If you did not deduct any depreciation, decrease the basis by the amount you could have deducted.

If you deducted more depreciation than you should have, decrease your basis by the amount you should have deducted, plus the part of the excess depreciation you deducted that actually decreased your tax liability for any year.

Fair market value defined

The fair market value of your home is the price at which the property would change hands between a buyer and a seller, neither having to buy or sell, and both having reasonable knowledge of all necessary facts. Sales of similar property, on or about the date you begin using your home for business, may be helpful in determining the property's fair market value.

Figuring the depreciation deduction for the current year.

If you began using your home for business before 2013, continue to use the same depreciation method you used in past tax years.

If you began using your home for business for the first time in 2013, depreciate the business part as nonresidential real property under the modified accelerated cost recovery system (MACRS). Under MACRS, nonresidential real property is depreciated using the straight line method over 39 years.

To figure the depreciation deduction, you must first figure the part of the cost of your home that can be depreciated, which is called the depreciable basis. The depreciable basis is figured by multiplying the percentage of your home used for business by the smaller of the following.

- The adjusted basis of your home, excluding the land, on the date you began using your home for business.
- The fair market value of your home, excluding the land, on the date you began using your home for business.

78. CAR AND TRUCK EXPENSES – SELF-EMPLOYED

For many small business owners the deduction for the business use of their vehicle is one of the largest business expense deductions. Due to the fact that this can be a large deduction plus the fact that many taxpayers try to inflate the amount of this deduction the IRS looks very closely at this deduction. IRS records show that 11.5 million Schedule C filers claimed the car and truck expense deduction in 2011. The average amount of the deduction for these taxpayers was almost $7,300.

If you use your car in your business and use it only for that purpose, you may deduct the entire cost of operation. But, if you use it for both business and personal purposes, you can only deduct the cost of the business use.

For most of your business expenses, the IRS doesn't require your documentation of the expense to be in a particular way. This is not the case with the car or truck expense deduction. With this expense the IRS details exactly what they want regarding documentation of the expense.

There are actually two ways to claim the car or truck deduction, you can claim your actual expenses or take the standard mileage rate.

Of course the IRS has some rules in place for who can and can't claim the standard mileage rate

Choosing the standard mileage rate

If you want to use the standard mileage rate for a car you own, you must choose to use it in the first year the car is available for use in your business. Then, in later years, you can choose to use either the standard mileage rate or actual expenses.

If you want to use the standard mileage rate for a car you lease, you must use it for the entire lease period. For leases that began on or before December 31, 1997, the standard mileage rate must be used for the entire portion of the lease period that is after 1997.

You must make the choice to use the standard mileage rate by the due date, including extensions, of your return. You cannot change this choice once made. However, in later years, you can switch from the standard mileage rate to the actual expenses method. If you change to the actual expenses method in a later year, but before your car is fully depreciated, you have to estimate the remaining useful life of the car and use straight line depreciation.

Information about Your Car

If you claim any deduction for the business use of your car, you have to provide certain information about the vehicle including:

- Date placed in service.
- Mileage (total, business, commuting, and other personal mileage).
- Percentage of business use.
- After-work use.
- Use of other vehicles.

- Whether you have evidence to support the deduction.
- Whether or not the evidence is written.

Standard Mileage Rate

If you qualify to use the standard mileage rate, the rate for 2014 is 56 cents per mile. If you use the standard rate for a year, you can't also claim your actual car expenses for that year. However, there are a few exceptions to this rule, in that if you are self-employed, in addition to the standard mileage rate you can still deduct:

• The part of the interest expense on a car loan that represents your business use of the car (the remainder is not deductible)
• The part of the personal property tax on your car that represents your business use of the car (the remainder is deductible if you itemize deductions), and
• Business-related parking fees and tolls.

Interest

If you are an employee, you cannot deduct any interest paid on a car loan. This applies even if you use the car 100% for business as an employee.

However, as a self-employed business owner if you use your car in your business, you can deduct that part of the interest expense that represents your business use of the car. For example, if you use your car 60% for business, you can deduct 60% of the interest on Schedule C. You cannot deduct the part of the interest expense that represents your personal use of the car.

Personal property taxes

If you itemize your deductions on Schedule A, you can deduct on line 7 state and local personal property taxes on motor vehicles. You can take this deduction even if you use the standard mileage rate or if you do not use the car for business.

As a self-employed business owner who uses your car in your business, you can deduct the business part of state and local personal property taxes on Schedule C, or Schedule C-EZ. If you itemize your deductions, you can also include the remainder of your state and local personal property taxes on the car on Schedule A.

Actual Car Expenses

If you do not use the standard mileage rate, you may be able to deduct your actual car expenses. If you qualify to use both methods, you may want to figure your deduction both ways to see which gives you a larger deduction.

Actual car expenses include:
- Depreciation
- Licenses
- Gas
- Oil
- Tolls
- Lease payments
- Insurance
- Garage Rent
- Parking fees
- Registration fees
- Repairs
- Tires

How to Prove or Document Your Expenses

As I mentioned earlier, unfortunately, due to widespread abuse by taxpayers, car and truck expenses are looked at very closely by the IRS. IRS regulations require that you keep a record in order to deduct your mileage, without a log, the IRS will disallow the deduction if you are audited. The good news is, the IRS tells us exactly the type of documentation they are looking for. They even provide an example of a log, with the information they are looking for.

Your mileage log should include the date the car was used for business, the destination, the business purpose, the beginning and ending odometer readings, the miles for each business trip, and if using actual expenses, the amount of the expense and what it was for. I suggest that you also note in your log the odometer reading at the beginning and end of each year.

This log should be done contemporaneously, or as soon as you make each business trip. You shouldn't go back and try to create a log at the end of the year. The IRS prefers that you keep your log on paper and in ink, rather than electronically because it is harder to fabricate paper logs. However, you do have the option of using an electronic log and the IRS is supposed to accept it. For those of you who prefer a more high-tech approach, there is an app for iPhones called Mileage Log+. The app will track the miles you drive and you can enter the business purpose for each trip and according to the latest information I have, it is considered IRS compliant.

One method IRS auditors use to catch taxpayers who try to create their mileage logs after-the-fact, rather than recording the information as the car is used, is to check the odometer records that are recorded each time your car is serviced. There is a record of what the odometer reading is each time you buy tires, or have your oil changed, or have your state inspection performed. If the odometer reading in your mileage log for a certain date doesn't match what is listed when one of these services is performed, then the IRS will disallow your vehicle mileage expense deduction for the entire year.

If you drive about the same amount for business throughout the year, you may be able to use the sampling method instead of keeping track for the entire year. I personally do not recommend this, as it increases the risk of having your deduction being disallowed.

However, if you decide you want to use the sampling method, here are the things you need to keep in mind. You will still need to keep a log with the same information recorded, but instead of doing so for the entire year, you only do it for part of the year. Keep in mind that the sample period must be at least 90 days long. You then use the figures for the sample period and extrapolate the business mileage for the entire year.

This method assumes that you drive about the same amount for business throughout the year. To backup this assumption, you have to keep meticulous records of your appointments. So, you are trading one record keeping requirement for another.

As I stated, the sample period must be at least 90 days long. It could be the first 90 days of the year, or the first week of each month. It doesn't even have to be the first 90 days or first week of the month. Whatever works best for you, as long as it is as representative as possible of the business miles you drive during the year. You must keep track of the total miles driven during the year by recording the beginning and ending odometer readings.

79 . PARKING FEES AND TOLLS

Many people who choose to use the standard mileage deduction instead of the actual car expense method mistakenly think that they can't include any additional items related to the business use of their car.

However, in addition to using the standard mileage rate, you can also deduct any business-related parking fees and tolls. However, if you have claimed depreciation on your car, you can't deduct tolls or parking fees as well.

In addition, the parking fees you pay to park your car at your place of work are considered nondeductible commuting expenses.

80. TRAVEL, MEALS, & ENTERTAINMENT

The travel expenses for the purposes of this chapter are for out of town travel, not local travel which is included in your car or truck expenses that we discussed in the previous chapter. To determine whether you can deduct your out of town travel costs you have to determine whether you are considered to have a tax home.

Let's look at how you determine if you have a tax home. Usually, your tax home is your regular place of business, regardless of where your family home is. You can have a tax home even if you don't have a regular or main place of business. If you answer yes to all three of the following questions, your tax home is where you normally live. If you answer yes to two of the questions, you might have a tax home depending on all the facts. If you only answer yes to one of the question, you are considered a transient, and you can't deduct travel expenses.

Here are the questions to determine your tax home:
- Do you conduct part of your business in the same area as your home where you spend the night?
- Do you duplicate your living expenses when you are away from that home for business?

- Do you often use that home for lodging, or have a member of your family living in that home?

How often and for what reason you have out of town travel will vary widely from business to business. A common reason for out of town travel expenses in some industries is business conferences. If you travel for a conference and the conference is purely for business you can probably deduct the expenses.

You have to be able to show that attending the conference benefits your business. It can't be for political, investment, or social reasons. If the convention is outside of North America, you can only deduct the expenses if you can show that there was a good reason for it being out of the country.

In addition, if the conference is out of North America, then, you can't spend more than a week, and at least 75% of the time has to be business related. The IRS knows that many people who attend conferences take some time off to relax or add on some days to do some sightseeing. There is no problem with that, but you can't claim any of the personal expenses as business deductions.

If the trip requires overnight stays, then the costs of lodging is also deductible. Meals are also deductible, as long as they are not considered "lavish" to use IRS terminology. However, you can only deduct 50% of the cost of meals. Other incidental business expenses like fax charges or renting time on a hotel computer, or taxi fees are all deductible as well. Travel costs for employees are also deductible, but costs for family members are not.

The IRS shows that the average travel expense deduction for the 4.2 million taxpayers, who claimed the deduction, was a little over $3,000. This is an expense category where you will want to keep copies of all receipts and keep good records so that you can prove the expenses are legitimate to the IRS if necessary.

81. MEALS

For 2011, 4.2 million taxpayers claimed meals and entertainment expenses as a business deduction, with the average amount totaling just over $2,000. Let's look at meal expenses more closely. There are two circumstances which allow you to deduct a portion of the costs of meals.
- If it is necessary for you to stop for substantial sleep or rest to properly perform your duties while traveling away from home for business, or
- If the meal is business-related entertainment

In this section I'm just going to talk about meals that are NOT business related entertainment, we will talk about those a little later.

As I mentioned earlier, you can't deduct expenses for meals that are lavish or extravagant. The IRS doesn't set a fixed limit on the cost of a meal before it is considered lavish or extravagant. All facts and circumstances are considered. Just because a meal expense exceeds a certain dollar limit or takes place at an expensive restaurant or resort will not disallow the expense.

You can compute your meals expense using either the actual cost or using the standard meals allowance. Regardless of which method you use, generally you can only deduct 50% of the cost of your meals. The 50% limit applies whether the meal expense is for business travel or business entertainment.

Actual Cost Method

You can use the actual costs of your meals and multiply by the 50% deduction limit to compute the deduction amount. If you use this method you must keep records of the actual cost.

Standard Meal Allowance

Generally, you can use the standard meal allowance method as an alternative to the actual cost method if you don't want to keep records of your actual costs. This method allows you to use a set amount for your daily meals and incidental expenses. The amount varies depending on where and when you travel. Even if you use the standard meals allowance, you still have to keep records to prove the time, place and business purpose. You just don't have to have receipts to prove the amount of the expense.

The current standard meal allowance ranges from $46 to $71 per day. Most places are $46 per day, with the higher rates applying in major cities and other higher cost locations. These rates can change and you should check the most recent General Services Administration (GSA), publications to determine what rate you should use. The rates can also be found at www.gsa.gov/perdiem. You can enter the zip code or city that you traveled to, for the current rates.

Travel for Day You Depart and Return

On the day you leave on a business trip and the day you return from a business trip, you must prorate the standard meal allowance. You can use one of two methods:
- You can 75% of the standard meal allowance
- You can prorate using any method that you consistently apply and that is in accordance with reasonable business practices

Example

Sam is a real estate agent in Dallas. He attends a business conference in Atlanta. He leaves his home at 10 am on Wednesday and arrived in Atlanta at 5:50 pm. After spending two nights in Atlanta, he flew home on Friday arriving at 8 pm.

Under Method 1, Sam can claim 2.5 days of the standard meal allowance for Atlanta, ¾ of a day for both Wednesday and Friday, and a full day for Thursday.

Under Method 2, Sam can use any method that he applies consistently and that is in accordance with reasonable business practice. He could claim 3 days of the standard meal allowance.

82. TRIP PRIMARILY FOR PERSONAL REASONS

If your trip was primarily for personal reasons, the entire cost of the trip is a nondeductible personal expense. However, you can deduct any expenses that you have while at your destination that are directly related to your business. The scheduling of incidental business activities during a trip such as attending lectures dealing with general topics, will not change what is really a vacation into a business trip.

This is an area where you need to be careful, some trip promoters advertise trips to their resort or cruise ship as business trips. In some cases that may be true, but if they are really vacations in disguise, don't try to claim the deduction.

For example, let's assume you schedule a conference in Orlando, and you take your family with you. While there you and your family go to Disney World every day. You also do spend a couple of hours attending the conference on several days. If the conference is business related, the cost of the conference is probably deductible. However, the travel costs probably would not be given the information I provided. Since the main purpose of the trip was personal.

83. ENTERTAINMENT

You can deduct entertainment expenses only if they are both ordinary and necessary and meet one of the following tests. The Directly-related test, or the Associated Test, I will go into these tests a little later.

An ordinary expense is one that is common and accepted in your business. A necessary expense is one that is helpful and appropriate for your business. An expense doesn't have to be required to be considered necessary.

Directly-Related Test

To meet the directly-related test for entertainment expenses, including entertainment related meals, you must show that:
- The main purpose of the combined business and entertainment was the active conduct of business
- That you did engage in business with the person during the entertainment period, and
- That you had more than a general expectation of getting income or some other specific business benefit in the future.

Associated Test

Even if your entertainment expenses don't meet the directly-related test, they may meet the associated test. To meet this test you must show that the entertainment is:
- Associated with the active conduct of your business, and
- That it is directly before or after a substantial business discussion.

Generally, an expense is associated with the active conduct of your business if you can show that you had a clear business purpose for having the expense. The purpose may be to get new business or encourage the continuation of a business relationship.

Whether a discussion is substantial depends on the facts of each case. However, you do need to show that you actively engaged in the discussion or meeting to get income or other specific business benefit.

Entertainment Expenses That Are Not Deductible

There are certain types of entertainment expenses that you are not allowed to deduct. These include: club dues and membership fees; any expenses for the use of an entertainment facility; which includes things like a hunting lodge, fishing camp, swimming pool, bowling alley, or vacation resort.

As you can see there are many different types of expenses that may be deductible within this category of expense, however, like many other deduction, the rules are complex, and you need to understand that if you don't follow the IRS guidelines these expenses will not be allowed.

CONCLUSION

I hope I have been able to provide information that has been useful to you in legally minimizing the amount of taxes you have to pay. I know I haven't included every topic, and I know haven't gone over every single detail for the topics that I have covered.

I have tried to balance providing enough information to be useful without overwhelming you with all of the details. If you have a question about something, please feel free to contact me via email or phone. I will be happy to try to assist you.

I can be reached toll-free at (888)505-6592 or via email at info@premiertaxresolution.com.

ABOUT THE AUTHOR

Danny Fink is a veteran accountant and tax expert who specializes in providing tax advice and tax preparation. He has a Master of Science degree in Accounting from James Madison University, he is a CPA licensed in both Virginia and West Virginia. He is also a member of the American Society of Tax Problem Solvers and is licensed to represent taxpayers before the IRS in all 50 states.

He first began in the tax business almost 30 years ago by preparing tax returns. He is the owner and founder of Premier Tax Consulting. One of the leading tax firms in West Virginia.

He is a long-time endurance athlete, and was a member of the United States Summer Biathlon National Team for ten years, and represented the United States at eight World Championships, winning two medals in International competition as a member of Team USA.

He now uses the same drive, and commitment to excellence, that he used to become a world-class athlete, to help his clients with their tax issues.

Fink's first book, *The IRS Offer in Compromise: Uncle Sam's Let's Make a Deal Program*, became the top selling book on the subject on Amazon within the first month of release. His second book, *The Real Estate Agent's Tax Guide*, is widely considered the "go-to" resource for Real estate agents with tax questions.

www.ingramcontent.com/pod-product-compliance
Lightning Source LLC
Chambersburg PA
CBHW051701170526
45167CB00002B/487